DATE DUE

DEMCO 38-296

THE NEW FINNISH ARCHITECTURE

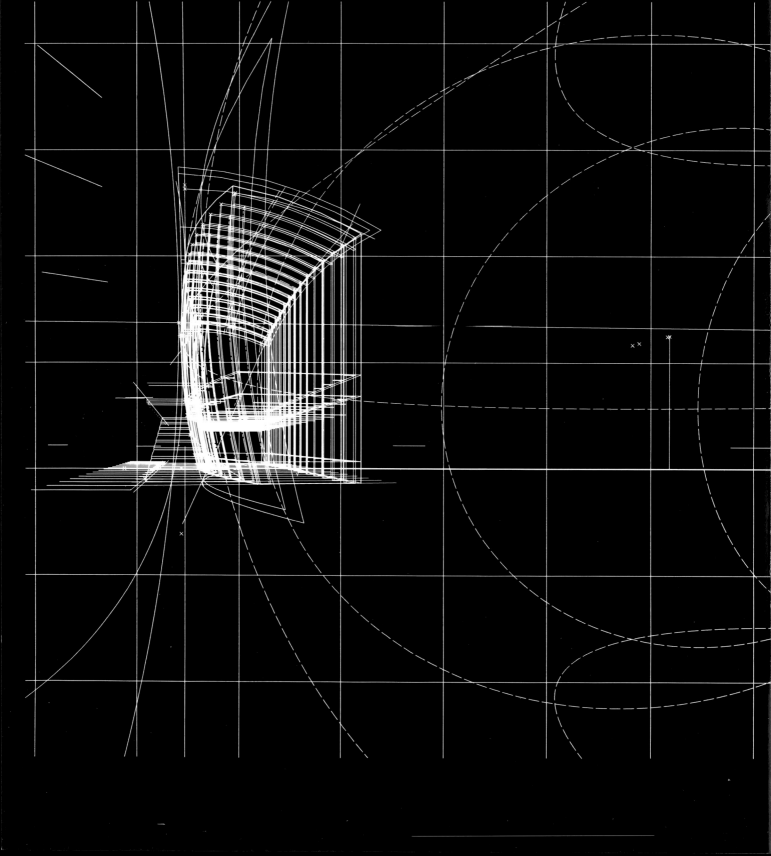

THE NEW
FINNISH ARCHITECTURE

By Scott Poole

Introduction by Colin St. John Wilson

First published in the United States of America in 1992
by RIZZOLI INTERNATIONAL PUBLICATIONS, INC.
300 Park Avenue South, New York, N.Y. 10010

Library of Congress Cataloging-in-Publication Data

Poole, Scott.
    The new Finnish architecture / Scott Poole: introduction by
Colin St. John Wilson
    p.   cm.
    ISBN 0-8478-1316-9 (HC) —ISBN 0-8478-1317-7 (PB)
    1. Architecture—Finland.   2. Architecture, Modern—20th
    century—Finland.   I. Title
NA1455.F5P66   1992   91-12431
720'.94897'0904—dc20   CIP

Designed by Paul Chevannes
Set in type by Graphic Arts Composition, Philadelphia, Pa.
Printed and bound by Tien Wah Press, Singapore

Front cover: Mikko Heikkinen and Markku Komonen, Heureka: The
    Finnish Science Center, Helsinki, 1988
Back cover (hardcover only): Mikko Heikkinen and Markku Komonen,
    Heureka: The Finnish Science Center, Helsinki, 1988
Frontispiece: MONARK, Computer-aided design study for the Finnish
    1992 World Exhibition Pavilion, Seville, 1991

To the Memory of Alvar Aalto and Aulis Blomstedt

Acknowledgments

Generous support for the production of this book has come from the National Endowment for the Arts, the Graham Foundation for Advanced Studies in the Fine Arts, and the American-Scandinavian Foundation.

I wish to thank, in particular, the staff of the Museum of Finnish Architecture: Marja-Riitta Norri, director; Sirkka Valanto, head archivist; Tiina Nivari, Laura Tuominen, Elina Standertskjöld of the archive department; and Anna-Lisa Amberg, curator.

I would also like to thank Robert Gerloff, Victoria Larson, Clara Cox, and Kaarin Taipale for their editorial advice.

For their assistance obtaining photographs, I am grateful to Marja Pystynen, Artek; Kaija Ravanti, Form-Function-Finland; Tony Parkkina, Museum of Applied Arts; Veikko Pakkanen, Art Museum of the Ateneum, Helsinki; Satu Ahonen, Hackman-Iittala Oy; Kira Reuter, Arabia Finland Oy; Vesa Takala, Ikonifoto Ky; Elsi Mattila, Welcome to Finland; Risto Kinnunen, Muuramen kunta, Sirkku Dölle, National Board of Antiquities; Minnami Hatakka, Stockman Oy; Göran Schildt, Alvar Aalto Archives; and Tapio Laine Kodak Oy, Helsinki.

I would also like to express my gratitude to the Fulbright program of the United States and the Finnish Ministry of Education for their support in 1983–84 during my year of study in Finland.

The following individuals were especially helpful: Veikko Bonsdorff, an extraordinary patron of architecture, for unselfishly offering his time to show me several buildings he had commissioned; William Copeland for his assistance when he served as director of the U.S. Educational Foundation in Finland; Professor Salahuddin Choudhury of VPI for his perceptive advice on readings; Anna Jäämeri-Ruusuvuori for the kind use of her studio; Merja Niemi for her friendship; Chris Jeffrey, Jim Powers, and Amy Wilson for their graphic work.

I am especially indebted to Juhani Pallasmaa for giving straightforward criticism, for sharing his wisdom and knowledge, and for never attempting to influence the direction of this book.

I also must acknowledge Colin St. John Wilson for graciously accepting my invitation to write the introduction for this book.

Without the encouragement and confidence of David Morton, senior editor at Rizzoli, Professor Kenneth Frampton of Columbia University, and the Rizzoli editorial board, this project would not have been possible.

Lastly, I must thank my students for their inspiration and patience.

Arto Sipinen, Cultural Center, Espoo, 1989

Contents

Foreword

Architecture is not merely national but clearly has local ties in that it is rooted in the earth. Through its forms it can achieve an international influence.

—Alvar Aalto

The two essays that follow the introduction to this book present mirror images of Finnish architecture. The first essay examines Aalto's sensuous, archetypal approach to modern architecture and the second examines the highly structured artistic framework for reconciling architecture and industrial culture put forward by Finland's rationalist architects. Following the essays, the new architecture is presented beginning with Aarno Ruusuvuori, who began building in the 1950s, and ending with the MONARK group, whose first building will be completed in 1991.

To this day the art of building in Finland remains inseparable from one name: Alvar Aalto. In the 1930s his architecture, furniture, and glass objects brought unprecedented international attention to Finnish architectural and industrial design. For nearly half a century, until his death in 1976, Aalto dominated the image the world had formed of Finnish architecture. Terms such as eclectic, irrational, regional, organic, and romantic have often been applied to his work, and, due to the fact that Aalto was such a dominant figure, his architecture has perpetuated a conventional image of Finnish architecture that has lasted into our time.

The conventional image of Finnish architecture as an art bound to a region dominated by cultural romanticism and personal expression has been reinforced over the past generation by the works of Reima Pietilä. In the 1980s his work received much critical acclaim, especially in the Anglo-American architectural community, where postmodernism was a dominant artistic force. But in Finland it would not be unreasonable to say his formal influence was minimal.

Without doubt, regional insularity and romantic thinking were important factors in establishing Finland's national identity in the early part of this century. But these aspects of Finnish artistic culture have been consistently exaggerated and over time they have become part of a sentimental image that only obscures the varied nature of contemporary Finnish architecture. The intellectual impediments formed by an overemphasized romantic position were already an issue at the turn of the century in Finland. In their pamphlet "Architecture: A Challenge to Our Opponents," of 1904, Gustaf Strengell and Sigurd Frosterus argued for an architecture of calculated reason to balance what they perceived as the arbitrary fantasy of National Romantic forms. As Strengell wrote, "We have plenty of decorative and 'artistic' talent here in Finland at present. What we need is some guiding, clear and rational force."[1]

The nostalgia for romanticism in Finnish culture was challenged in the second half of the twentieth century by a movement of rationalist architects led by Aulis Blomstedt. Through an international outlook and a filter of reason, they altered the art of building in Finland.

When rationalism emerged in the early 1950s, twenty years of modern architecture in Finland had been interrupted by five years of war and another five years of recovery and reconstruction. But the tradition of modernism endured—a fact that is particularly significant considering that 80 percent of Finland's building stock has been constructed since the time of its independence in 1917.

In 1950 modernism was still a fresh idea. But rationalism was a new force, an artistic direction clearly in opposition to Alvar Aalto's more personal approach. For the past two generations the rationalist architects who worked within this new movement, along with their students and former assistants, have had a profound and often underestimated effect on the theoretical as well as formal development of Finnish architecture.

Establishing a sense of architectural identity apart from Aalto was a great difficulty for architects who began their careers after World War II. Juhani Pallasmaa, one of the leaders of the generation that worked in the shadow of Aalto, recently wrote, "During his lifetime Aalto's artistic identity was so strong that instead of creating a wide school of followers in his own country his impact gave rise to an opposite view of architecture. It is rather typical that great personalities have both centripetal and centrifugal effects." He went on to say, "Among the young generation his impact gave rise to a cast concrete minimalism inspired by Le Corbusier, a Bauhaus elementarism and a constructivist classicism which was inspired by Mies as much as by traditional Japanese architecture and the California rationalism of Craig Ellwood, Pierre Koenig, Charles Eames, Rafael Soriano and others."[2]

In the past twenty years the architect's role in Finnish culture has been severely questioned by Finnish society. Beginning in the years following the Paris student revolution of 1968, there was a collective loss of faith in the significance of architecture. In these times of technocratic thinking, especially in the 1970s, even the architects themselves occasionally lost sight of the optimism of the modern movement and the ideals of their own profession. The artistically unambitious housing and office complexes from this era are vivid reminders of a time when Finnish society had become skeptical of one of the fundamental qualities of architecture—its potential as a source of well-being.

In retrospect the 1970s seem to have been an unfortunate time for both Finnish architecture in general and for Finland's rationalist architects in particular. It was a time when there were many opportunities for building, but only rare chances for architecture. Ironically, key figures within the constructivist component of the rationalist movement hardly participated in the built environment of the 1970s, yet they have, on occasion, been blamed for the diminished vitality of the architecture of that era.

During that period, leaders of the rationalist school placed themselves at the forefront of the theoretical debate in Finnish architecture and headed the country's architectural institutions. Kirmo Mikkola, for example, became editor in chief of the Finnish architectural review *Arkkitehti* in the late 1960s; in 1975 Aarno Ruusuvuori succeeded Kyösti Ålander as director of the Museum of Finnish Architecture; and in the early 1970s Juhani Pallasmaa directed the School of Industrial Design in Helsinki, where the masters Tapio Wirkkala and Kaj Franck had taught, and he later became director of the Museum of Finnish Architecture.

The honorary position of state artist professor has been awarded to only five architects by Finland's president: Reima Pietilä, Kirmo Mikkola (who passed away in 1986), Aarno Ruusuvuori, Juhani Pallasmaa, and Kristian Gullichsen have each held this honorary title and all, with the exception of Pietilä, who abandoned a rationalist approach by the late 1950s, became the vanguard of the Finnish constructivist and purist movements in the 1960s. These architects are just now reaching the peaks of their careers as their opportunities to build increase along with their international exposure.

Rather than focus on the already widely published, unique forms and personal expressions found in the work of Reima Pietilä, the new architecture presented in this book focuses largely on the universal approach favored by Finland's rationalist architects whose search for structural order, simplicity, and elemental purity has dominated the theoretical discourse in Finnish architecture for the past thirty years. Also included, however, is the work of several architects who have developed strong modernist positions somewhat outside of Finnish rationalism. For example, Juha Leiviskä, an architect who builds transparency with walls and the modulation of light, would perhaps only fit an expanded rationalist category. In fact, he has been identified in the press as a follower of the Aalto school, but he prefers to be linked with the teaching of Aulis Blomstedt.

New thoughts within Finland's tradition of modernism are also represented in this book by a younger generation of architects whose most recent designs build on a tradition of Finnish architecture that has yet to be recognized internationally—a tradition that I would call silence. Like the eyes of a saint in an orthodox icon, the plainness of certain time-worn peasant objects, or the empty black window of an abandoned farmhouse, silence is an active force in Finnish architecture. More than the acuteness of silence in the dark, this silence is deep, it pervades its object and suggests a force outside the object.

Markku Komonen and his partner Mikko Heikkinen are two architects whose most recent designs realize Finland's tradition of silence in the art of building. In a work such as their recent display pavilion in the Netherlands, there is a depth of silence. "Deep silence," wrote the philosopher Bernard P. Dauenhauer, "appears not to flow but to abide. . . . Deep silence shows itself as more prominent than the utterances which serve to maintain it."[3] Komonen, it should be added, worked in close collaboration with Aarno Ruusuvuori and Juhani Pallasmaa when he held the position of director of the exhibitions for the Museum of Finnish Architecture. He also served as editor in chief of *Arkkitehti* from 1977 to 1981.

Significantly, all of the architects presented in this book practice in Helsinki. The capital city is the locus of energy for the production of architecture in Finland. In the past, the vast majority of Finland's significant buildings were drawn in the offices of Helsinki's architects and this is still the case today. With the exception of Pentti Kareoja and the architectural team ARRAK, all of the architects presented in this book were educated at the Helsinki University of Technology (TKK) and all were trained in the classes and offices of architects who themselves had been educated at the TKK. Their architectural positions range from the strict, unwavering constructivism that Erkki Kairamo has practiced for the past thirty years to the naïveté of Georg Grotenfelt's recent modernist regionalism.

With the exception of the MONARK group, who have not yet completed their studies at the TKK, each of these architects is a teacher in the sense that a critical aspect of a Finnish architect's training is formulated in professional offices, where the education of a young architect is taken as a serious responsibility. Typically, students graduate from the TKK approximately ten years after they begin their professional studies, with time nearly equally divided between formal curriculum and professional experience. Surprisingly, it is in the office and not the classroom that the most experimental and innovative work often occurs in Finland.

In all of Europe there is perhaps no other nation that concentrates such a large proportion of its resources on the architects of a single city. Recently, for example, a planning competition was held for the Kamppi-Töölönlahti section of central Helsinki. In only the first stage of this ideas competition over two hundred thousand dollars were shared by the three architects who divided the first prize. In another open competition for the extension of a major commercial building in the center of Helsinki, over sixty thousand dollars was awarded to the first-prize winner and the next four places shared over one hundred thousand dollars. All were architects from Helsinki.

The center of Helsinki is small. One can literally

walk from Eliel Saarinen's train station at the northern edge of the city center to the sea at the city's southern rim in fifteen minutes. The concentration of so much architectural talent in such a small area leads to a remarkable dialogue between the architects there.

In the past, Finland's physical location on the fringe of Europe allowed this dialogue to remain somewhat removed from international trends in architecture. Concentration and isolation had at one time allowed Finland's architects to assimilate outside influences slowly and critically. But in recent years the mass media has had an increasingly adverse effect on Finland's architectural culture. This effect is adverse because it dismantles one of Finland's most precious qualities—remoteness.

Remoteness had allowed Finnish architecture to maintain what Martin Heidegger calls nearness. In his influential book *Poetry, Language, Thought*, Heidegger discusses the fatal loss of distance in the modern world and makes this unsettling remark: "Despite all conquest of distances the nearness of things remains absent."[4]

For centuries, Finland's distance has encouraged nearness. In the arts it has allowed objects to gather presence, and it has provided time for discriminating thought. Postmodernism, for example, had very little impact on Finnish architecture in the 1980s, but it seems that postmodernism as well as new forms of uncontrolled expression might be more difficult to resist in the 1990s, due to the seductive imagery of mass communication.

In Finland, architects have maintained a position of great prestige due in large measure to the social responsibility embedded in the tradition of their art. At its highest level, this responsibility includes insuring that architecture as a source of well-being is not comparable to the thought of architecture as a commodity.

Finnish architects have been able to maintain a sense of social responsibility in their art, even in the most difficult times, because they have a structure that protects the artistically strong. This structure is supported by an extraordinary competition system that virtually guarantees architects a forum for fresh ideas and a venue for untried talent. In Finland it would be difficult to name many significant buildings erected after 1900 that did not result from a competition, and it would be equally difficult to name a prominent Finnish architect whose career did not begin, was not highlighted, or was not sustained through architectural competitions.

Competitions and the results of competitive efforts have nurtured talent and protected dreams. They have given young architects the opportunity to test their designs, which occasionally win. In 1989 an open competition was held for one of the most prestigious commissions awarded in Finland in recent years: the Finnish Pavilion for the 1992 Seville World Fair. The competition entries included many of Finland's most talented architects, but the first prize was awarded to a team of five students who were in the first years of their architectural training at the Helsinki University of Technology. Their success in this important competition only confirmed the implicit intention of one hundred years of architectural competitions in Finland—that excellence will not go undiscovered.

Competitions insure that, from the moment they begin their studies, Finnish architects' lives are filled with hope. In addition to competitions, the critical role of enlightened clients cannot be underestimated in Finnish architecture. Individual patrons, industry, and the state have accepted and even promoted modern architecture. Without such support the continuity of modernism in Finland would have been impossible to maintain.

One such client, Maire Gullichsen, born into a prominent industrial family, was a tireless advocate of modern art and architecture for over half a century. She and her husband, the industrialist Harry Gullichsen, not only commissioned the house that is the subject of the first essay in this book, but she also founded Galerie Artek and, along with Aino and Alvar Aalto and Nils Gustav Hahl, began the Artek Furniture Company. With her death in the summer of 1990, Finland lost a pioneer of modernism and an individual of rare foresight.

Industry has also supported ambitious programs of architecture. A fine example would be the Valio dairies, which have commissioned a number of exceptional office and industrial facilities over the past fifteen years.

In the 1990s the state may begin to perform a larger role in sustaining the vitality of Finnish architecture than it has in the past. In 1985 Matti K. Mäkinen, who was educated at the height of constructivist thinking and was one of the country's leading architects in the 1970s, was appointed director general of the National Board of Public Building. His background as an award-winning designer and his high expectations have already changed the course of some state commissions. For Mäkinen, average is no longer tolerable when architects build for the state. It is their duty, he believes, to be creative.[5] His office is in a unique position to have a positive influence on Finnish architecture in the last decade of this century.

In the 1990s the reconciliation of the sensual and intellectual aspects of this tradition and, in particular, the reintegration of Aalto's work within the architecture of a generation of designers who at one time only wanted to escape his shadow will be a fascinating development.

NOTES

1. Sigurd Frosterus and Gustaf Strengell, "Architecture: A Challenge to Our Opponents," *Abacus* 3 (Helsinki: Museum of Finnish Architecture, 1982), 65.
2. Juhani Pallasmaa, "Finnish Architecture after the Paris Spring and Alvar Aalto." Lecture delivered at the International Conference on Architecture, Urban Planning, and Design, Espoo, Finland, September 6, 1989, typescript page 3.
3. Bernard P. Dauenhauer, *Silence: The Phenomenon and its Ontological Significance* (Bloomington: Indiana University Press, 1980), 16–24.
4. Martin Heidegger, *Poetry, Language, Thought* (New York: Harper & Row, 1975), 166.
5. Matti K. Mäkinen, interview with the author, July 6, 1989.

INTRODUCTION

Finland and the Tradition of Modernism

Colin St. John Wilson

A Sense of Heritage

IT HAS been said that the greatness of the innovator can be measured by the extent to which he hinders progress after his death. Any approach to the architecture of Finland has to consider the application of this proposition to Alvar Aalto, who most certainly was one of the discipline's great innovators. However, the content of this book alone belies the charge of rigor mortis: I know of no livelier body of work anywhere else in the world. It should be understood that Aalto's predominance is more an impression held outside Finland, because of his great international reputation, than a constituent factor in the unfolding of Finnish architecture. As we shall see, other native talent and interpretation have indeed influenced the work illustrated here even more than Aalto himself.

Finland, it seems, is the one country in which the architecture of the modern movement has developed without challenge and come to maturity as if in its natural habitat. For the Finns, modernism has so matured that it has achieved the depth of perspective proper to a tradition of its own. On one level this is a simple fact of life, for in Finland only one building in eight is older than sixty years. At the level of architectural polemic, it is significant that an architect like Kristian Gullichsen, when he jestingly confesses to "a taste for clichés (as long as they are good ones)," does not have in mind the recollections of the Arch of Constantine or the Villa Malcontenta so much as references to Le Corbusier, Aalto, Sigurd Lewerentz, Johannes Duiker, and Adolf Loos. In a later note he refers to "the tradition of sixty-five years of modernism" and goes on to say, "It is my conviction that this intellectual and artistic base contains an inexhaustible source of architectural concepts, rich in meaning and history; in short, it is a gold mine which it would be foolish not to explore." In other words, for Finnish architects the modern movement is not only an unchallengeable foundation for an evolving architecture, but has, during the last sixty-five years, established an ample tradition.

How is this so? It lies in the chemistry and history of a culture, and that is an infinitely complex phenomenon. One might as well ask why Greek culture posed the sort of questions that could only be answered by the invention of entasis, and then pursued the consequences of that answer with the intensity of a moral imperative. At a happy moment in history, the self-awareness of a growing nation somehow became encoded and embodied in architecture. The moment was happy because it coincided with the genesis, emergence, and self-realization of a worldwide revolution in the experience of architecture; and that sense of a new beginning, of *L'Esprit Nouveau*, seems to have been seized upon as one of the principal roots of identity and sources of imagination in the formation of a whole culture.

From this, there has come into being a quality of rootedness in the realm of *res publica*. This is a gift beyond price when compared with the position in Great Britain or the United States, where it is necessary to drum up an apologia for every building's "meaning"—a scarce resource in a public vacuum. This phenomenon was not the achievement of a single man nor of a single generation, but something sustained by many talents across a broad range of values. Certainly Aalto and his wife, Aino, were the first off the mark, setting up their practice in the same year as Le Corbusier: 1922. But it was in the context of a lively range of international contacts, both personal and institutional (Congrès Internationaux d'Architecture Moderne), that Finnish architecture put itself on the map. Neither England nor the United States provided any comparable engagement or contribution to the give-and-take of innovation and promotion, of practice and polemic, that we now identify as the great modernist adventure of the 1920s and 1930s. By comparison, the architectural culture of Finland (in which the constructivism of Russia was as active as the classicism of Sweden, and the purism of Paris as provocative as the new objectivity of Berlin) from the late 1920s onward grew contemporaneously with the original innovations. And in so far as Aalto, Erik Bryggman *(1)*, and Yrjö Lindegren contributed their own inflections to that rapidly evolving language, the claim by the current generation of architects in Finland to draw upon that tradition has the simple authority of a birthright. Furthermore, it is not a right based only upon those better-known (and certainly well-advertised) contributions, but contains from its earliest formation the strands of great diversity.

This quality of diversity has to be emphasized if one is to do justice to a debate that has been sustained for the last thirty-five years in the publication of *Le Carré Bleu* (1958–69) and subsequently in the yearbook *Abacus*. For instance, one would not have been prepared for the selection of Tadao Ando for the Aalto Award in 1985 unless one were aware of the background of elemental abstraction in the very influential work and teaching of the "rationalist" Aulis Blomstedt and the equally authoritative minimalist school of Ruusuvuori *(2)*, Pit-

1. Erik Bryggman, Resurrection Chapel, Turku, 1940

2. Aarno Ruusuvuori, Weilin & Göös Printing Works, Tapiola, Espoo, 1964

känen *(3)*, and others. And this debate has been vigorously and eloquently argued ever since, particularly in the writings of Juhani Pallasmaa and the late Kirmo Mikkola.

Finnish modernism has always been a complex affair. Simply to take into account Aalto's Villa Mairea is to realize that it is an architecture that has very little to do with the International Style, that purely stylistic formula promoted by Hitchcock, Barr, and Johnson after a tourist trip to Europe in 1932. The irrelevance of that formula (no decoration, no history) to the richly narra-

3. *Pekka Pitkänen, Cemetery Chapel, Turku*

4. *Gunnar Asplund, initial competition design for the Stockholm Public Library, 1921*

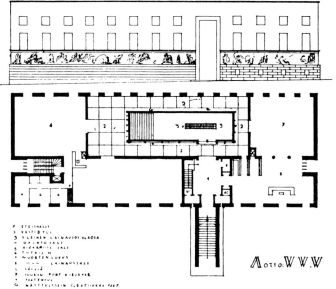

5. *Alvar Aalto, elevation and plan, Municipal Library, Viipuri (now Vyborg, USSR), 1928*

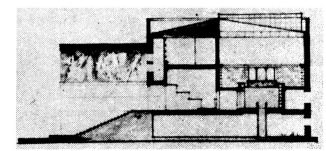

6. *Alvar Aalto, section, Municipal Library, Viipuri (now Vyborg, USSR), 1928*

tive form of the villa has been most convincingly spelled out by Demetri Porphyrios. By the same token, Finnish modernism has little reason to take too seriously postmodernism, whose terms of reference are merely the reversal of those postulated for the International Style (all decoration, all historical quotation). Indeed, the Finnish response to postmodernism broadly takes three forms: a very decisive relationship to the classical tradition, an inexhaustible capacity to extend the language of form, and an uninterrupted commitment to symbolic reference wherever appropriate.

The Relationship to Classicism

In its unequivocal view of the relationship between modernism and classicism, Finland has the advantage of sharing in the very positive attitude to that tradition adopted by the Nordic countries earlier in this century. This is eloquently demonstrated by the line of thought that developed through two closely related buildings. The story begins in 1921 with the competition entry by Gunnar Asplund for the Stockholm Public Library. In the initial project for this building, a round reading room (embracing three levels in stepped-terrace form) is entered at the head of a long, ascending staircase *(4)*. That stair, in turn, is approached directly from an entrance portal of exaggerated vertical form. Most of the paraphernalia of classical language (dome and Corinthian portico) were shed in the eight-year course of the project's development, but the main elements in plan and section were retained in stripped geometrical form. In particular, the tall portal and the ascending stair retain

their force as figurative elements in the complete building of 1928. Aalto's competition project for the Viipuri Library (1928) is an extremely sophisticated spatial invention which nevertheless acknowledges its lineage in the Stockholm Library *(5, 6)*. The asymmetrically placed

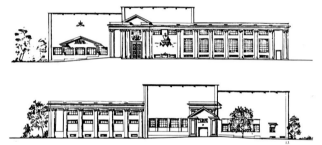

7. *Alvar Aalto, elevations of final design, Municipal Library, Viipuri (now Vyborg, USSR), 1935*

8. *Viipuri Library, revised elevations proposed by the Russians, 1952. (courtesy Viipuri City Archives)*

portico, flanked as in Stockholm with reliefs of classical provenance, cuts through a rusticated base, affording entry by a long, ascending staircase to the reading room, as in Asplund's library. The resemblance, however, does not stop there. For just as Asplund's project evolved from an explicitly Palladian prototype into a neoclassicism that stopped only just short of the functionalism of his 1930 Stockholm Exhibition pavilions, so did the Viipuri Library develop (once again over eight years) through three stages. In this case the final version (built in 1935) arrived at the modernist experience *pur sang*; that is, forms were no longer derived from precedent (be it Palladio or Asplund) but from patterns of use. For the control of daylight upon the page, the distribution of circulation systems, and the acoustic performance of the lecture room, unprecedented forms were invented.

This revival of classicism was seen not as a nostalgic turning back to the past but as a stepping forward into modernism. But there is a sting to this tale. In 1952 the Russians considered a project for "the renovation of the building on the basis of modern Soviet architecture." In their proposal, the façades of the Aalto building were to be plastered with Ionic columns and pilasters *(7, 8)*. This is precisely what the classical revivalists of today would wish to do, and the irony lies in the discrepancy between the linguistic crassness of those who are attempting to revive what Edwin Lutyens rather pompously called "the high game" of classicism and the brilliant inventiveness of those who have abandoned it. It is surely not without significance that the few architects who have

added a genuine footnote to the development of neoclassical language in this century (one thinks particularly of Lewerentz and Asplund) abandoned that language because it could no longer say what had to be said. We could profitably recall Le Corbusier's broadside in *Vers une architecture*: "Rome is the damnation of the half-educated."

Enlarging the Language of Modernism

As to the capacity of the modernist language to sustain further development, the claim by the philosopher Jurgen Habermas that the modernist adventure is an "unfinished project" is given substance by the fertile inventiveness with which the architects represented in this book continue to affirm, hone, and extend the language they have inherited. While elsewhere so many had accepted the modernist language as just a "style" (the International Style), in Finland functionalism was truly addressed as a root-and-branch social idea. As early as 1940 Aalto pointed out, "It is not the rationalization itself which is wrong in the first and now past period of modern architecture. The wrongness lies in the fact that the rationalization has not gone deep enough. Instead of fighting rational mentality, the newest phase of modern architecture tries to project rational methods from the technical field out to human and psychological fields . . . . The present phase of modern architecture is doubtless a new one, with the special aim of solving problems in the humanitarian and psychological fields." And where this is the case, the grounds for a development of language are not so much syntactic as pragmatic.

However, at the level of syntax, it is a common virtue of all the work in this book that it is in the handling of light that new life is brought to all the elements of that language—wall, column, frame, ceiling, equipment. Once again Aalto set the pace. He said of his Aalborg Museum *(9)*, "Light is to the art gallery what acoustics are to the concert hall," and he made of that building an instrument as delicate and precise as a Stradivarius violin; within it light was molded, filtered, reflected upward from trays of shimmering water, and directed downward or obliquely to reveal sculpture or painting to its best advantage: living light, not "engineer's light."

For Gullichsen, who shares Le Corbusier's passion for the wall and the "subtle, precise and magnificent

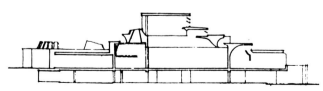

9. *Alvar Aalto and Jean-Jacques Baruel, cross sections, Aalborg Museum, Aalborg, Denmark, 1972–76*

10. *Kristian Gullichsen, Kauniainen Parish Center, Helsinki, 1979*

11. *Juha Leiviskä Myyrmäki Church and Parish Center, Helsinki, 1984*

play of forms in light," light is the medium of what Adrian Stokes called the "carving mode." In Gullichsen's Kauniainan Parish Center *(10)*, one is reminded of Stokes's reference to Palladio's "vivification of wall space."

For Juha Leiviskä, light is not carved but (again in Stokes's phrase) "modeled" by means of planes overlapping in rhythmical sequences of layers, like cubism that seems to hold all forms suspended in a radiant levitation. In his churches *(11, 12)*, the physics of light becomes the metaphysics of light: as Abbot Suger wrote in his poem on the chapel of St. Denis, "per lumina vera ad Verum Lumen" (through clear lights [windows] to the True Light).

Erkki Kairamo draws his inspiration from a different concern within the modernist canon—the frame structure of industrial fabrication. In his work it is not so much a preoccupation with technology per se that confronts us as the jolting energy of constructivism, the buoyant and colorful rhetoric of optimism. Unpredictably, this mode works as convincingly in his residential

12. *Juha Leiviskä, Myyrmäki Church and Parish Center, Helsinki, 1984*

15

13. *Erkki Kairamo, Liinasaarekua 3–5 Semidetached Houses, Westend, Espoo, 1980*

In the work of Simo and Käpy Paavilainen there is an extraordinary tension between a spatial distribution so dynamic that for comparison one would have to look to Hans Scharoun and a tendency for the component parts to reveal an ancestry, however remote, in classical antiquity. Simo Paavilainen is a scholar-architect who has thought deeply and written well about the Nordic classicism of the 1920s. What is gratifying in his approach is that it eschews the symmetries and bombast so dear to postmodernism and draws instead upon the oblique sensibility that we find in the *Erechtheion* or the temple site at Pergamon. As with Le Corbusier, it is to the Greek, not the Roman, that he responds. In the parish centers of Olari *(15)* and Kontula *(16)*, we encounter a radical freedom from conventional axiality resulting in the kind of aperspectival space that is the only way to make sense of a grouping of activities that at times de-

14. *Erkki Kairamo, Itäkeskus Tower and Commercial Center, Helsinki, 1987*

15. *Käpy and Simo Paavilainen, Olari Church and Parish Center, Espoo, 1981*

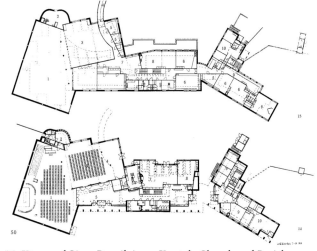

16. *Käpy and Simo Paavilainen, Kontula Church and Parish Center, Helsinki, 1988*

buildings at Westend, Espoo *(13)*, as in his office and commercial complex in Helsinki *(14)*. The spirit of his work is closer to that of Duiker who, in his Zonnestraal ("ray of sunlight") Sanatorium, proclaimed that "the hygiene of light, sun, and air say good-bye to the Middle Ages forever!"

16

mands absolute separation and at others seeks to share a common space.

The Question of Symbolic Form

Walter Gropius's assertion that the language of modern architecture is radically cut off from the past has never been without challenge in Finland. We have already alluded to the complexity of the Villa Mairea. It is not surprising therefore that Kristian Gullichsen (who was raised in that house) should have no difficulty responding to the narrative and iconological aspects that demanded resolution in his Kauniainan church. His handling of the modernist canon is both supple enough to cope with a very complex topographical context and subtle enough to embody appropriate elements of symbolic form. The representational intent is sustained at a number of levels and is quite without strain. Allusions are made both to antiquity as well as to the immediate past, but they are not made to "hot up" the style nor merely to borrow authority from the past. They are simply arrived at as a result of thinking through the real relationships at issue, and in so doing rediscover themes found there either two thousand or twenty years ago. If, therefore, the west wall undulates, it does so—much as it did with Borromini or Lewerentz or Aalto—to find a place for a font, a sacristy, or a stair; if the rising topography introduces a difficulty in building the main floor level of the church into the hillside, Gullichsen's choice of a descending approach also recalls the catacomb of the primitive church. The four columns in the church can be said to symbolize the four evangelists, the three light wells and the triangular skylight over the altar to represent the Trinity, and so on. In the same way, Leiviskä admits to a passion for the interiors of Bavarian rococo churches, yet transcribes their inexplicable splendor of white and gold into a completely new language, free from the need for any direct quotation.

Conclusion

All in all, the status of contemporary architecture in Finland constitutes a certain reproach to the reactionary nostalgia, the dithering and scuttling, the lost sense of common purpose, and the instant kitsch that dominate the scene and are fostered elsewhere by those whom Habermas has rightly stigmatized as "the Avant-Garde of the Great Retreat." It is not without some envy that we note how in Finland the architectural profession has won an enviable position of public confidence. Certainly I know of no place in which revivalism and postmodernism have made less inroad upon the claim to orthodoxy of modernism than Finland. I suspect that the prevalence and rigor of the competition system in Finland have much to do with the generally high level of design that leads to such confidence. Virtually all public buildings and many other buildings are the subject of competition. I suggest that the role played by women architects has a lot to do with this success, for, either as partners in a man-and-wife team (one thinks of Heikki and Kaija Sirén, Alvar, Aino, and Elissa Aalto, Reima and Raili Pietilä, and Simo and Käpy Paavilainen) or solo (from Signe Hornberg and Wivi Lönn to Kaarina Löfström), the contribution of women is very significant.

And so we salute the unruffled persistence with which in Finland the potentialities of the modernist adventure are being broadened and deepened; and above all the fact that such a broadening is based upon an unquestioned belief in the sufficiency of resources deployed by the modern movement, which has by now its own tradition.

MODERN ARCHITECTURE IN FINLAND: TWO ASPECTS

ELEMENTAL MATTER IN THE VILLA MAIREA

Scott Poole

How many painters, lacking that special sensibility called for by the mysteries of water, harden the liquid surface until, in Baudelaire's phrase, "the ducks swim in stone"!
—Gaston Bachelard

"So the twentieth century is that," wrote Gertrude Stein in 1938, "it is a time when everything cracks, where everything is destroyed, where everything isolates itself; it is a more splendid thing than a period where everything follows itself." That same year, 1938, Alvar Aalto completed his drawings for the Villa Mairea, and Gertrude Stein was concluding her text on Picasso with these words: "Everything destroys itself in the twentieth century and nothing continues."[1]

To describe the Villa Mairea as a construction of heterogeneous elements that have been removed from a context, displaced in time, recomposed, compressed in layers, and held together with paste—is to evoke an image of this experimental house as collage. Alvar Aalto noted in his text on the villa that the form concept included "a deliberate connection to modern painting."[2]

One only needs to look at the works of the analytical cubists to see a world that has been fractured, torn, and pulled apart—a world no longer capable of sustaining the unity of a single structure. And if, as Gertrude Stein suggests, discontinuity and fragmentation are among the aspects of life that are most relevant to our century, then the tearing, overlapping, interpenetration, and superimposition of collage were the inevitable means to reveal such a time. Or so it seems in retrospect.

The fragments that have been gathered for the construction of the Villa Mairea seem to have been chosen on the basis of their potential for confrontation and antipathy rather than out of a desire for uniformity and consistency. It is as if Aalto wanted to prove that opposites coexist. One might even say that a prime criterion for the selection of these elements was a certain distance—not so much a spatial distance, but a distance in texture, manufacture, material, and, most especially, time.

It would be a mistake to think that the multiple awareness that Aalto creates in this house is merely an indication of an avant-garde mentality. The disparity between the elements of the villa and their strange adjacencies may have the surrealism and irrationality of a dream, but the desire to resolve the difficult opposition between the archaic and the modern was often driven by one basic question: What is eternal in the contemporary?

The Metaphysics of Timelessness

Throughout the Villa Mairea, the new, the unique, and the modern are juxtaposed with the traditional, the archaic, and even the primordial. But there is a hierarchy in the coexistence of these disparate categories; it would be more accurate to say that the new is embedded in the old. Concrete and steel are rarely allowed to assume a dominant figural quality in the composition of the house. Where modern materials are visible they are typically neutralized or partially concealed and fall into the background *(17)*. Glass, for example, is often dominated by wooden frames, exterior blinds, or a view of earth, water,

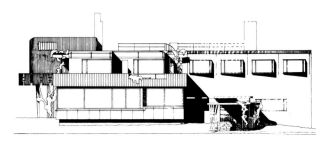

17. *Alvar Aalto, southeast elevation, Villa Mairea, Noormarkku, 1938–39*

and trees. Exterior walls formed by industrially manufactured bricks are covered by white paint and stucco in such a way that their materiality is obscured and even denied. For Aalto, the memory of a traditional use or the sensual qualities contained in a material were essential to the layers of imagery he formed in the villa, but materials with a short history and at times even the medium of architecture itself were often subservient to form.

Modern techniques and materials may be suppressed in the house, but their presence animates the remote in time. Ordinary and humble fragments from common vernacular buildings—the fence, the porch, the sauna, and the large, undifferentiated main room of the Finnish farmhouse—are juxtaposed with sheets of plate glass, rolled steel, and poured concrete. In this unfamiliar context the naïve and simple are seen as they have never been seen before. They become objects of contemplation.

Parts of the villa are assembled in such a way that a fragment can be seen as nothing more than what it is— a sod roof, a steel column, a wooden post, a glass wall, or a concrete beam—and simultaneously, virtual leaps through time can occur when the mind begins to reconstruct a whole from these elements. In these elements with a past, and in their position and relation, there is a suggestion of a future.

The fragments with which Aalto builds are restructured with little regard to classic propriety or chronological time, but obligations to adjacency do exist. Everywhere in the Villa Mairea those things that are contemporary to our century are positioned to reverberate with that which is timeless in a house. And as deeply as the villa is bound to the material, to the sensual, and to things that are forever becoming, the immaterial and unchanging aspects of its form allow it to oscillate between this instant and eternity.

Collage Construction and the Ontology of House

In an essay written during the construction of the Villa Mairea, Aalto expressed admiration and possibly envy for the circumstances of building in ancient times:

One could perhaps call the art of architecture during these primitive times an "art of discovery." Because of the lack of possibilities for processing, it was imperative to find ready-made building materials in nature. Blocks of stone, tree trunks, and animal skins were perhaps the likeliest choices and the art of architecture was a matter of combining them correctly.[3]

The "primitive" technique Aalto describes bears a striking resemblance to the manner in which he was constructing the villa. The house seems to have been understood as an unchanging, ontological entity that could sustain a ceaseless flow of memories and images initiated by new relations among existing elements. In their singularity these fragments of a house—a glass window, a wood sauna, a stone path, a garden gate—disclose little of significance. But through layering and superimposition, through the "art of discovery" and correct combination, the construction materials and the images created by them have the capacity to inspire reverie, an aspect fundamental to the existence of a house.

Significantly, Aalto noted in this regard, "Buildings materials and construction methods do not by themselves exert a one-sided and direct influence on architecture."[4] The collection of materials that Aalto employs in the collage construction of the Villa Mairea may appear strange and unrelated, but the form of the villa has universal qualities. Its interiority refers to something essential inside all of us. When we dwell anywhere we hide within. The unforgettable house in the imagination contains our innermost recesses. It protects intimacy and makes room for solitude. It sustains silence. And its nearness can make the world seem vast.

Memories of interiority can last a lifetime, and even the most modest house can provide us with a refuge from the world and enclose well-being. In his meditations on images of intimacy, Gaston Bachelard, who can find inspiration in the depth of almost any humble home, tells us that "the house is one of the greatest powers of integration for the thoughts, memories and dreams of mankind."[5]

The house of memory is milk for the imagination of a philosopher like Bachelard. "When we go to live in the house of Memory," he tells us, "the real world vanishes all at once."

What are the houses on our street worth compared to the house of our birth, that house of total interiority, which gave us our sense of inwardness? That house is remote, it is lost, we no longer live in it, we are only too sure that we will never live in it again. And so it is more than a memory. It is a house of dreams.[6]

The continuous construction of inwardness in a house that is more than a memory gives order to the seemingly arbitrary in the Villa Mairea. As an entity, the villa is new, yet at the same time unspeakably old. The relations among its parts are relations of recovery in which memory resists forgetting and the lost qualities essential to the inner nature of a house are repossessed in the form of archetypal reverie.

Architecture and Elemental Matter

The materials taken from the modern world of the engineer and the scientist are challenged throughout the Villa Mairea. The imprecision of hand-made forms are set against the precision of the machine-made. The shiny is flattened by paint, tubular steel columns are mummified by cane and glistening black lacquer, concrete is covered with layers of earth and grass, and thin metal balusters are concealed by the thick primitivity of wood rails that have been cut and stripped of their bark. All over the house the new is consumed by the old. It is flattened, mummified, covered, and concealed.

While the materials Aalto employed are products of the earth, those that have been dug from the ground, melted, rolled, cooled, and significantly reformed are given a lesser status than those that have hardly been touched by the process of manufacture. The wood Aalto used in the construction of the villa is almost exclusively the product of industrial processing, yet the primeval memories associated with an uprooted tree often dominate the imagery of the house. Aalto's wood has the familiarity of thousands of years of well-being.

Fire, water, earth, and air assume a critical position within the arrangement of the house's parts. Their inseparability from archaic building traditions gives a

sense of authenticity to the construction of the Villa Mairea. This enduring relationship between house, humankind, and the elements recalls the depth of a past that has been preserved in the Finnish mind since ancient times.

Akseli Gallen-Kallela brings this form to the visual world in his 1903 painting *Rakennus* (Building) *(18)*. In this idealization of an eternal human condition, Gallen-Kallela brings us close to the landscape of the Finnish soul. On the land and near some water a family constructs its home. Rocks, trees, and the floor of the earth are the only protection. From the womb of the mother is a suckling child and in the womb of the house under construction there will be a shell for the family. This primordial image stirs within us the primitive feeling of the earth as a feminine being. It recalls memories of well-being and arouses dreams of protection, security, and intimacy.

18. Akseli Gallen-Kallela, Rakennus, *1903*

The house embraces itself in the painting. It folds on itself and is coiled around a core. Each log is an enclosure that takes us inside, away from the caprice of the elements and into the protectiveness of walls. The image reminds us that we are bound to the earth, that we are sustained by the earth, and that the human mother only repeats what the earth already knows.

The hope and hopelessness contained in the act of construction is painfully apparent in Gallen-Kallela's painting. Ruin and death are the inevitable fate of building and dwelling. Yet the hand, the ax, and the precision of the caliper endlessly repeat the possibility of life that nourishes the art of building.

While this painting certainly contains a sentimental invitation to a romantic age when man and nature lived in harmony, it is not all idealization and unrestrained nostalgia. The sustenance of dwelling made vivid by this image only reminds us of the haunting loss of home in the modern world.

Archetypes and Repetition

In the Finnish national epic *The Kalevala*, the creation of the world begins with a woman. This primordial archetype of feminine creation is repeated endlessly in the warm humidity of the Finnish sauna *(19)*. Perhaps nowhere in architecture is the union of the elements as strong as it is in the darkness of this wooden vessel. In the closeness of its dilated air, where stones from the earth are activated by fire and animated by water, we bathe in more than moist heat and soft light. Saturated by water and surrounded by wood, we bathe in the warmth of our own well-being.

19. *Traditional Finnish sauna, Muurame, Central Finland*

This cosmos of wood that has the atmosphere of warm water suggests a world of unusual unity where the primal elements and their intimate warmth give us a palpable sense of the roundness of life. One could argue that Aalto found a pattern for a house hidden in the images of this exemplary model. It could even be said that a paste of water and earth bound the Villa Mairea's collage of fragments into a single form.

In the eighteenth century, the chemist Herman Boerhaave wrote of water's will to bind in *Chemistry of Elements*:

Even stones and bricks reduced to powder and then exposed to the action of Fire . . . always give a little water; and they even owe their origin in part, to Water, which, like glue, binds their parts together.[7]

Some of Aalto's sketches as well as his formal compositions in stone suggest an origin in an element as formless as water, and they appear as naïve as Boerhaave's chemistry. In the winter garden a floor of stones floats in a mortar of burned and powdered minerals bound to water. Near the wooden sauna *(20)* and at the front entry to the villa, stones bathe on the surface of the earth as if they had forgotten that they were heavy matter.

That Aalto should find glue for his collage in water imagery was hardly unusual. Water is essential to the Finnish poetic imagination and in the past it gave rise to a tradition. The mythological force contained in water was at the core of the fragmentary poems from which Elias Lönnrot constructed the epic *The Kalevala*. Lönnrot's reflections on the etymology of the hero Väinämöinen's name reveal the depth that water plumbs in the Finnish imagination. He wrote in 1839:

Perhaps, initially, the discussion in this entire creation tale may not have been about Väinämöinen, but rather about "Vein emonen" (Mother of Waters). "Emo, emäntä, emonen" (Mother, Mistress of the House) was the general term for that from which each substance derives its sustenance, solidity, strength.

Lönnrot goes on to say that *"Vein emonen"* might be understood as something more than a female goddess and could more generally be seen as *veden ylläpitäjä* (one who sustains the water) or even *veden omituinen voima eli juuri* (the water's unique power or root).[8]

20. *Alvar Aalto, exterior view of sauna, Villa Mairea, Noormarkku, 1938–39*

Water and the Material Imagination

Aalto wrote of his desire to experiment with material and surface treatment in his description of the genesis of the Villa Mairea. More precisely, these were experiments in depth. "Great ideas arise out of the small details of life," he later wrote. "They spiral out of the earth."[9]

Water in combination with the earth was a primary source for Aalto's imagery in the villa. But water was often a dominant element in Aalto's material imagination. In the mid-1930s in particular, Aalto revived nineteenth-century *Kalevala* romanticism with images that implied that the architect could be "one who sustains the water."

The curvilinear line that dominates the Finnish landscape as well as Aalto's glass, furniture, sculpture, and architectural designs of the 1930s *(21–24)*, is clearly

22. Alvar Aalto, Paimio Chair no. 41, molded plywood, 1931–32

21. Finnish landscape c. 1893, Sortavalato looking south from Riutanvuori Hill (now Lake Ladoga, USSR)

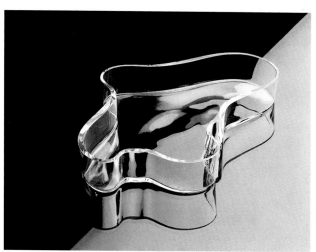

23. Alvar Aalto, glass tray, Karhula Iittala Glassworks, 1936

24. Alvar Aalto, laboratory experiment with laminated wood, c. 1931

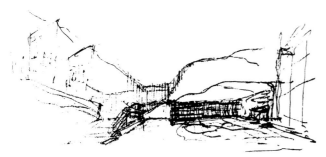

25. Alvar Aalto, conceptual sketch of the main hall of the Villa Mairea, Noormarkku, 1938–39

evident in his sketches for the Villa Mairea. In one sketch the main room of the house is drawn as flowing, nourishing water *(25)*. In this imprecise image of depth and distance there is an elusive vision of a house. It is an image of concentrated primitivity in which Aalto recalls, in the fleeting moment of a dream, the slow, rocking monotony of liquid matter; it brings back times, close to the twentieth century, when the whole of Finnish life was immersed in wood—in the cradle, in the wooden farmhouse, and in the forest.

Almost without exception in the villa, wood is applied as a covering or skin with qualities of temperature and accumulations of time that were associated with memories of warmth and well-being. Aalto makes no effort to conceal the ornamental role of wood in the house. Near the foyer layers of pole screens hang from the walls and stairs, recalling the formless depth of the Finnish forest. In the main room, wood carpets the floor and covers the concrete ceiling. And on the exterior wood is ornamentally applied to structural elements wherever a textural effect is desired.

In an essay written in the 1950s, Aalto recalled the opposition between the snow that surrounded the courtyard of his house at Muuratsalo and the flames of a winter fire that burned at its center. Under the influence of the flame's reflections in the surrounding snowbanks, he remembered "a pleasant, almost mystical feeling of warmth."[10] It was this warm feeling that he longed to recover in the wood that sheathed the Villa Mairea.

Aalto understood the hard coldness of concrete, steel, and glass. He knew their conductivity and disliked their hunger for heat.[11] But in the depth of wooden matter he found the fecundity of fire and the water of life, two elements that permeate ancient Finnish myths and the sensual imagery of the sauna.

Water, Fire, and Wooden Matter

In all of Aalto's architecture there is perhaps nothing more pervasive than his desire to resolve seemingly irreconcilable contrasts. Aalto wrote that the way in which the writer August Strindberg placed opposites against one another "hints at the manner in which art and the

purely material world may be united." Aalto further wrote, "In every case we must achieve a simultaneous solution of conflicting problems."[12]

In the plan of the Villa Mairea *(26)*, the water of the courtyard is surrounded by fires. In the living room, in the sauna, and on the outer wall of the dining room, the flames of these fires seem to be more alive when compared to the calm look of the courtyard's tranquil water. Even unlit and cold, they suggest in their individual plans a union of opposites in which a repetition of three right-angled walls holds three fires and the curves of three fluid forms. The tension that occurs between these straight lines and soft curves, and the anticipation of fire in front of water, is heightened by the inflections of each hearth. The wood platform of the sauna drinks the water of the plunge pool, the stone of the outdoor fireplace is inflected toward the water, and a cavity with curves that long to hold water *(27)* is carved out of the wall of the living-room fireplace. To speak of feminine creation in the presence of so much pregnant matter would only be redundant.

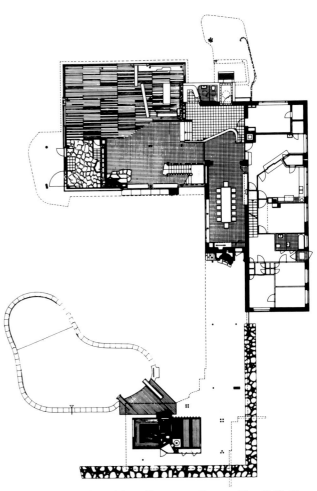

26. Alvar Aalto, plan of the Villa Mairea, Noormarkku, 1938–39

27. *Alvar Aalto, fireplace detail facing courtyard, Villa Mairea, Noormarkku, 1938–39*

which has little to do with thought forms, we are reminded of Bachelard's maxim: "Dreaming reveries and thinking thoughts are certainly two disciplines which are hard to reconcile."[13]

There is an abundance of evidence in Aalto's writings, objects, and buildings which suggests that he desired to remedy the overemphasis on formalism that he perceived in modern architecture and design. "The contact with nature and its constantly observable change is a way of life that has difficulty getting along with concepts that are too formalistic,"[14] Aalto wrote in 1935. Throughout the Villa Mairea, there is a vivid sense that concepts could only crush its images.

The fundamental thoughts that underlie Gaston Bachelard's phenomenological studies of the imagination were being developed at the same time that the Villa Mairea was being designed. Bachelard's thesis that the origin of an image can grow directly out of matter seems to have been shared by Aalto, who had simultaneously manifest this idea in his works.

In a fascinating essay on the Spanish artist Eduardo Chillida, Bachelard writes that the "cosmos of iron is not an immediately accessible universe. To approach it one must love fire, hardness and strength." Chillida's constructivist abstractions from the 1950s dare our eyes to penetrate the surface of matter. He cultivates our imagination with his passion for iron. Bachelard suggests that in Chillida's works the forging of iron "asserts initiatives of its own" and that it unfolds in the manner of an "autonomous growth." He says, "Chillida's iron is nobody else's iron. This remarkable smith really does dream dreams of iron, he draws with iron, he sees with iron."[15]

Indeed, it would be difficult not to imagine warm water in the midst of so many fires and so much liquid matter, perhaps as difficult as it was in olden times—when the Tree of Life drank the earth's water and held the blood of the sun in its marrow—not to recognize the sun's flame in a flowering tree.

Reverie and Thought Form

Aalto's meditations on the inner life of elemental matter take us to the root of an image. Water, fire, and the warmth of wooden substance suggest a world beneath the surface in the villa *(28)*, a world that provides access to the primordial source of water's unique power or root implied by the myths of *The Kalevala*.

The sensual texture of the main room of the house depends upon the formlessness of liquid images and their power of dislocation. Here the feeling aroused by matter gives impulse to the imagination. In this room, the tangible strangeness we feel is the intimacy of elemental matter and its primitive invitation to the feeling of nature. One only has to open the door to this house to understand that Aalto is awakening us into a dream. In this dream,

28. *Alvar Aalto, front portico, Villa Mairea, Noormarkku, 1938–39*

If we were to substitute Chillida's love of fire, strength, and hardness for the water, warmth, and softness that Aalto awakened in wood, we might better understand the alchemical passion the artist and the architect shared. We might even believe that only adoration can penetrate matter. Aalto's imagination was immersed in wood. He drew dreams of wood as formless water. He sculpted water in wood. His impulse to bend wooden matter with soft liquidity was an obsession. In Aalto's wood the murmur of water is everywhere.

Can there be any doubt of Aalto's intention to animate elemental matter in the Villa Mairea? Certainly he is not suggesting a return to a primitive state of nature feeling, but at the same time his work is a convincing argument that science does not have the capability to understand those aspects of elemental matter that only an artist can know. Who other than an artist can render with material a world that is not there?

D. H. Lawrence, in his book *Apocalypse*, reminds us of the limits of science: "All that science has taught us about fire does not make fire any different." For Lawrence, the four elements of Empedocles were established in the consciousness of humankind forever.

The processes of combustion are not fire, they are thought-forms. H_2O is not water, it is a thought-form derived from experiments with water. Thought-forms are thought-forms, they do not make our life. Our life is made still of elemental fire and water, earth and air: by these we move and live and have our being.[16]

It is important to note that Lawrence is not denying culture, he is merely asking us to recognize elemental matter as a force in our lives and to question the false wholeness of scientific determinism. Lawrence mourns the loss of a vital cosmos and is discouraged by the lack of depth in the modern intellect. "Our conscious range is wide," he writes, "but shallow as a sheet of paper."[17]

Like Lawrence, T. S. Eliot observed the thin consciousness of modern culture in his poem "The Rock":

Where is the Life we have lost in living?
Where is the wisdom we have lost in knowledge?
Where is the knowledge we have lost in information?[18]

Aalto too revealed his distress with the pervasive substitution of technical information for primordial admiration, when he wrote in 1935 that the contemplation of "the candle's yellow flame" offers us a kind of knowledge unknowable to the "electrical technician with his lux-meter and his schematic concept of 'white light.'"[19]

The Future of Eternity?

Speaking of the bond between the world and the human soul, Gaston Bachelard writes, "There lives within us not a memory of history but a memory of cosmos. *Times*

29. *Alvar Aalto, view across plunge pool, Villa Mairea, Noormarkku, 1938–39*

when nothing happened come back."[20] These are the times that Aalto recalls in the Villa Mairea, times of infinite repetition when the life of an archetype had the confidence of a thousand deaths.

Often the creative tension in Aalto's architecture came precisely from a struggle to recover the thin thread of continuity between his own time and a beginning outside of time *(29)*. And, on occasion, it is apparent that Aalto really does tear us away from history. Unlike so many architects of the avant-garde, he recognized the tragedy of forgetting. Aalto understood that fresh creation could have origins in remote sources, and his work seems to be most profound when it rehabilitates images at the core of archetypal models and in the depth of elemental matter.

In his desire to be periodically released from the bond of historical time and returned to an origin that is timeless, Aalto resembles the man of archaic societies who is described by Mircea Eliade as living a dual existence in order to escape the time of the clock. For archaic man it was only through the archetypal act, when he suspended the time of his everyday existence and projected himself into mythological time, that he was truly himself and part of the cosmos.[21]

This image of a unitary reality bound to the forces of nature separates the man of archaic societies from modern man, who believes that only history and the machinery of modern life bind him to the world. "History," James Joyce wrote in 1922, "is the nightmare from which I am trying to awake."[22]

Eternal Repetition and the Sacrifice of the Self

The disconnection of modern man from the thought of a vital cosmos becomes painfully apparent when we look at the Villa Mairea. Aalto's recovery of archetypal images bound to elemental matter gives the Villa Mairea a sense of authenticity that is especially poignant in our time, when so few images touch the concrete world of the spirit.

Aalto clearly recognized that the detachment of modern man from the sensuous memory of matter had diminished our lives. His thinking in this regard is in distinct contrast to a modern world overwhelmed by the self-consciousness of perpetual invention, a dilemma C. G. Jung pointed out: "All modern people feel alone in the world of the psyche because they assume there is nothing that they have not made up."[23]

Archaic man accepted the paradox that in order to create he had to cease to be himself. Original creation lies in the repetition of the typical rather than the search for the individual. In this sense Aalto's use of archetypal gestures bound to matter recalls more the man of traditional societies than the modern man, who is characterized by a will to manipulate the world and a reluctance to make sacrifices.

In his penetrating analysis of cinema, *Sculpting in Time*, the Russian filmmaker Andrey Tarkovsky poignantly expressed the gravity of this difficulty: "Artistic creation demands of the artist that he 'perish utterly' in the full, tragic sense of those words."[24]

"Nothing old is ever reborn," wrote Alvar Aalto, "but it never really disappears either. And anything that has ever been always re-emerges in a new form."[25] These words, written in the year he completed his architectural studies and nearly twenty years prior to the completion of the Villa Mairea, characterize a relationship to time that recognized the authority of the past and the active presence of tradition. Aalto is implicitly writing about a world in which time and timelessness overlap, a world of repetition in which the eternal, in the words of the Danish philosopher Søren Kierkegaard, could be found in a "future that comes again like a past."[26]

Architecture and Silence

The thought of the past holding material for a recurrent future pervades the Villa Mairea. The silence that surrounds the rear window of the house *(30)* brings us close to a moment that is outside of time and untouched by history—an instant between memory and imagination. It is as if Aalto is awakening an inner reflection of a world with which we no longer have contact.

At the edge of this dark room and its light-filled clearing the most elemental materials enclose two women and their solitude. They are immersed in wood and saturated by an atmosphere of water, earth, and roots. All around them the forms resonate with the symmetry of round life. It is as though they are witnesses to the birth of an ordered and centered universe. But this is hardly a unity imagined through geometry. It has no arcs, yet it is fully round. The measure of the forms in this image has almost nothing to do with the certainties

30. Alvar Aalto, rear window facing courtyard, Villa Mairea, Noormarkku, 1938–39

of ideal mathematical proportion, or a single vantage point. Instead the forms are a measure of the human soul against a world of perpetual being. Nearness permeates the image. It embraces the forms like a vessel of silence and everywhere there is a sense of a moment poised between this instant and eternity.

Behind the women the tread of a stair is caught by a shadow and never lands on the floor. In the clearing in front of them, the floor of the earth has become the roof of a building and the water in the courtyard reflects an immense and reversible world. Its hypnotic gaze is a mirror for the imagination, a thoughtful eye that recalls vast human longing.

It is all motionless, but in some places—the bend of the tree, the curve of the handrail, and the anticipation of the woman standing in the threshold—the tension of frozen movement is almost unbearable. It is as if this moment had been prepared for the deep tremble of a heavy bell, something as absolute and timeless as pure sound.

Even the humble dwelling in the clearing recognizes the silence and has left the earth; it appears to have come into existence in the air with a quiet reluctance. Its simple forms are like the repetitive language of a primitive song. The Swiss philosopher Max Picard wrote about a song in which "language hardly dares to exist. It is already separated from silence but not yet sure of itself. It repeats itself continuously as if it wanted to learn how to live, and were afraid of disappearing."[27]

A Perfect Shell for People's Lives[28]

In the Villa Mairea, Aalto awakens something that has been lost in our world and reestablishes contact with an ancient sense of dwelling that is still alive in modern man. He imagines a world of original contemplations, a world enlarged by material cause.

We have the feeling that at some critical moment Aalto has left himself behind in this work and placed us in the shadow of an imprecise recollection. If his images touch our inner being, it is not because the architect has convinced us of the existence and importance of his private world. Rather, Aalto transcends his own imagination through the authority of archetypal patterns and the thousands of years of repetition contained in their forms. It is this contact with an invisible tradition that stimulates our reverie so deeply and profoundly.

In the mid 1920s, at the height of revolutionary thinking in modern architecture, Le Corbusier wrote that "we must rid our hearts and minds of all dead concepts with regard to the house."[29] Unfortunately, by the 1930s many live concepts were thrown out along with those that were quite dead. Le Corbusier had asked architects to purify their work with objective criteria. His metaphorical statement that "the house was a machine for living in" is a profound thought, inseparable from the house as a source of well-being, but it has often been realized in the most naïve and literal sense in our time.

Aalto, unlike so many architects of his age, sensed the loss of home in the modern world. He understood that the spirit of the modern age and innovations in technology were insignificant and even trivial events when measured against timeless themes. His architecture in the Villa Mairea is a return to the "impure" world of sensual nature, a world that often doubts the primacy of the intellect, but has utter confidence in the wisdom of centuries without writing.`

For Aalto, the house of memory and imagination had little to do with machine romanticism; it was instead a shell for dreaming in. In place of a fractured modern world, he suggests the existence of a living unity in the depth of matter. Aalto recalls the mythical power of images bound to elemental substance. From a stone or a tree he arouses the most primordial sensations. With water he binds a house to the earth. His will to dream of matter sustains the force of archaic tradition and reflects an awareness of a lost way of life. For modern man, Aalto's dreams are strange labors. Provocative as they are distant, Aalto's images visualize a world filled with cosmic wonder, where the imagination still contemplates things that never progress—a world that we hardly dare dream of anymore.

NOTES

1. Gertrude Stein, *Picasso* (London: B.T. Batsford Ltd., 1938), 49.
2. Aino and Alvar Aalto, "Mairea." (Reprint of an article from *Arkkitehti* 9, 1939), trans. Jonathan Moorhouse, Leena Ahtola-Moorhouse in *Villa Mairea* (Helsinki: Artek, 1982), 3.
3. Alvar Aalto, "The Influence of Construction and Materials on Modern Architecture," (1938) *Sketches*, ed. Göran Schildt, trans. Stuart Wrede (Cambridge: MIT Press, 1979), 60.
4. Alvar Aalto, "The Influence of Construction and Materials on Modern Architecture," (1938) *Sketches*, 60.
5. Gaston Bachelard, *The Poetics of Space* (Boston: Beacon Press, 1969), 6.
6. Gaston Bachelard, "The Oneiric House" (1948), *On Poetic Imagination and Reverie* (Dallas: Spring Publications, 1987), 98.
7. Herman Boerhaave, quoted in *Water and Dreams*, by Gaston Bachelard, trans. Edith Farell (Dallas: The Pegasus Foundation, 1983), 107.
8. Juha Y. Pentikäinen, *Kalevala Mythology*, ed. and trans. Ritva Poom (Indianapolis: Indiana State University Press, 1989), 143.
9. Alvar Aalto, "Culture and Technology" (1947) *Sketches*, 94.
10. Alvar Aalto, "Experimental House, Muuratsalo" (1952) *Sketches*, 116.
11. See Aalto's criticism of an intellectual idea in terms of sensory experience in his discussion of Marcel Breuer's tubular metal chair in "Rationalism and Man," (1935) *Sketches*, 47–48.
12. Alvar Aalto, "Art and Technology" (1955) *Sketches*, 127.
13. Gaston Bachelard, *The Poetics of Reverie*, trans. David Russell (Boston: Beacon Press, 1971), 177.
14. Alvar Aalto, "Rationalism and Man" (1935) *Sketches*, 51.
15. Gaston Bachelard, "The Cosmos of Iron," (1956) *The Right to Dream*, trans. J. A. Underwood (Dallas: Dallas Institute Publications, 1988), 39–43.
16. D. H. Lawrence, *Apocalypse* (London: Penguin Books, 1976), 106.
17. Lawrence, *Apocalypse*, 47.
18. T. S. Eliot, "The Rock," in *Selected Poems* (London: Faber and Faber, 1963), 107.
19. Alvar Aalto, "Rationalism and Man," (1935) *Sketches*, 50.
20. Gaston Bachelard, *The Poetics of Reverie*, 119.
21. "When the Scandinavian colonists took possession of Iceland, 'Landnama,' and began to cultivate it, they regarded this act neither as an original undertaking nor as profane human work. Their enterprise for them was only the repetition of a primordial act. The transformation of chaos to cosmos." Mircea Eliade, *The Myth of the Eternal Return* (London: ARKANA, 1989), 34–36.
22. James Joyce, *Ulysses* (New York: Vintage Books, 1986), 28.
23. C. G. Jung, quoted in *Ego and Archetype*, by Edward F. Edinger (New York: G.P. Putnam and Sons, 1972), 103.
24. Andrey Tarkovsky, *Sculpting in Time*, trans. Kitty Hunter-Blair (New York: Alfred A. Knopf, 1987), 39.
25. Alvar Aalto, from the essay "Painters and Masons" (1921), quoted in *Alvar Aalto 1898–1976*, ed. Aarno Ruusuvuori (Helsinki: Museum of Finnish Architecture, 1981), 69.
26. Søren Kierkegaard, *The Concept of Dread*, trans. Walter Lowrie (Princeton: Princeton University Press, 1957), 81.
27. Max Picard, *The World of Silence*, trans. Stanley Godman (Washington, D.C.: Regnery Gateway Editions, 1988), 150.
28. Alvar Aalto, "Town Planning and Public Buildings" (1966) *Sketches*, 165.
29. Le Corbusier, *Towards a New Architecture*, trans. Frederick Etchells (New York: Holt, Rinehart and Winston, 1960), 210.

THE CONSTRUCTION OF SILENCE

Scott Poole

The Constraint of Number

ALT THE height of Alvar Aalto's career a foreign architect visiting Aalto's Helsinki office innocently asked what module the office used in their designs. It is said that one of Aalto's chief assistants replied, "One millimeter or less."[1]

This response became one of the most ridiculed statements by the generation of architects trained at the Helsinki Institute of Architecture in the 1950s. In contrast to Aalto, who disdained the module, these young architects had more in common with the universal approach of French poet Paul Valéry, who said, "I can find nothing in the arts that captivates me more than the forms or phases of *transition*, the refinements of *modulation*. For me perfect modulation is the crown of art. But in our time, little importance is attached to this ideal of mine."[2]

In the years of shortage following the Winter and Continuation wars,[3] an intensive program of industrial reorganization significantly altered Finland's economy, which had, until 1950, depended upon forest industries for 90 percent of all the nation's exports. It was understandable that a culture with such an economy would support romantic traditions tied to agrarian and rural roots. But with the development of an economy that was more diversified and less dependent upon the forest as a source of sustenance, there was a radical shift in the Finnish population from rural areas to cities and a subsequent housing shortage. Postwar relocations from areas that had been ceded to Russia only added to the housing difficulties urban areas faced during the 1940s, increasing the pressure for change within Finnish society and eventually causing a reevaluation of the role of architecture within that society.[4]

Already in the 1950s, Finland's first building using prefabricated elements *(31)* was being constructed to the designs of Aarne Ervi, an architect trained in Alvar Aalto's office. In these years, and particularly from the late 1950s onward, as aspects of Aalto's architecture seemed to move toward a more personal expression, the postwar generation of architects found new sources of inspiration

31. Aarne Ervi, Porthania University building, Helsinki, 1952

Toward Absolute Clarity

To deny the superfluous with an architecture of absolute clarity was one of Blomstedt's highest aspirations. His austere and unadorned works are traditional in the sense that they epitomize an old Finnish proverb asserting that a thing is "better quite smooth than badly decorated." His works make contact with peasant traditions as well as the most severe classicism of the 1920s, but there is no room in his architecture for the nostalgic or the sentimental—his faith in the unfinished project of modernism was resolute.

Blomstedt was a functionalist, but he practiced functionalism in the highest poetic sense of the term. His architecture did not depend on material or program; it was not a product of technology or a search for new plastic form. Instead, Blomstedt was determined to create what he called a "primitively correct architecture"[6] that was free of the weight of pragmatism, that was useful but never determined by utility, and that denied superficial innovation (32). Above all, he desired to touch the spirit of man with the harmony of pure form.

32. Aulis Blomstedt, annex to the Workers' Institute, Helsinki, 1959

in an approach that relied on universals.

Leading this school of thought was Aulis Blomstedt, an architect who completed his classical architectural education at the Helsinki University of Technology eight years after Alvar Aalto. In contrast to Aalto's conception of architecture as inseparable from the body and the senses, Blomstedt's work aimed at purifying architecture through intellectual consideration. His architecture was a search for the artistically eternal in forms that were timelessly classical. Modular and proportional discipline were the basis of Blomstedt's architectural theory. The geometric and arithmetic system of measures he developed, based on divisions of the number sixty and intervals of classical music theory, were a physical manifestation of his belief that freedom could only be found in restraint, and that there was a world of harmony and beauty in number. "In the beginning there was measure," Blomstedt said in one of his last lectures.[5]

Asceticism, simplicity, and silence were essential to his idea of architectural form, and their presence in his works is convincing evidence that fundamental truth exists in art. Blomstedt sought the core of form in these eternal, invariant aspects of architecture and in his meditations on number and geometry.

In his view, architecture was an autonomous discipline. "Of all arts," Aulis Blomstedt wrote, "only music and architecture are completely abstract: they do not actually represent anything."[7] The relation of number, proportion, and scale were the intangible concepts from which he constructed form. The form of number, the proportion of one element to another, and the scale of man to the world and universe were the invariant elements in his architecture which resonate with the tension of the classic. "Cézanne was a great revolutionary in the history of painting," said Blomstedt, "but to my mind all the radical change he achieved in painting was based less in the peculiarities in his art than on what was pictorially eternal in it, the artistically normal, just that which is understood by the word classic."[8] Blomstedt believed that an architect could use the doctrine of classical, dimensional coordination in a manner similar to a painter's use of color. In this respect his architecture aspired toward what he termed "a higher degree form concept than the plastic."[9]

The design of the annex to the Workers' Institute in Helsinki *(33)*, in which Blomstedt used a proportional module as the basis for what he called a construction of "invisible cubes," illustrates his desire for an immaterial architecture of purity and precision.

33. *Aulis Blomstedt, annex to the Workers' Institute, Helsinki, 1959*

The Invariant and Universal

Blomstedt was an active theorist whose numerous writings and lectures on the modern and the classical in architecture challenged cultural romanticism with their international outlook. As a founder of the theoretical journal *Le Carré Bleu*, and in his work with the CIAM, he encouraged Finnish architects through his own example to participate more fully in the theoretical dialogue of international architecture.

It was inevitable that his theoretical position—which looked for the invariant and the universal, was essentially nonempirical, and had as its highest aspiration a classic unity—would provoke a response from Alvar Aalto, whose architecture was often conspicuously national, sensuous, empirical, and inspired by the par-

ticularities of life. In short, the difference between Blomstedt and Aalto was that between classic and romantic.

When Aalto said in 1958, "I don't write, I build. The Creator created paper for making architectural drawings on. As far as I am concerned, everything else is a misuse of paper,"[10] his comment was certainly aimed at the new theoretical direction promoted by Blomstedt. In spite of the challenge set down by Aalto, Blomstedt continued to work toward an objective theory of architecture that was verified by practice, one that denied an intuitive approach to an architecture in which a module could be one millimeter or less.

The industrialization that occurred during the postwar years was seen by Blomstedt as a positive phenomenon in that it was an opportunity to apply his theory of dimensional coordination to prefabrication *(34, 35)*.[11] Unfortunately, his optimistic hopes with regard to industrial standardization have yet to be realized in Finland, but there were significant advances made in this field by his former students and assistants, and his influence continues to this day.

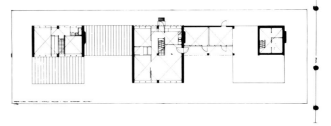

34. *Aulis Blomstedt, plan of Ketju and Kolmirinne Terrace Houses, Tapiola, Espoo, 1954*

35. *Aulis Blomstedt, Ketju and Kolmirinne Terrace Houses, Tapiola, Espoo, 1954*

Perhaps Blomstedt's greatest impact on Finnish architecture came during the years of his appointment as a professor at the Helsinki University of Technology from 1958 to 1966. During that period his theory and practice had an enormous influence on the generation of architects who are now reaching the peaks of their careers. He gave them the courage to make what exists better and the confidence that there was a future in modernism. But he also gave them something that is perhaps best explained in a passage from Dostoevsky's *Brothers Karamazov*. Blomstedt once cited the book in a lecture, recounting how Zossima, the monastery elder, has to answer the question "Is not the monastic system of modern times really an outdated and unnecessary institution?" Zossima explains, and Blomstedt recalled this from memory, "Their task in the Monastery is to keep pure and cherish the eternal truths, so that they would be at hand when mankind realizes the urgent need."[12]

Architecture and Emptiness

Rainer Maria Rilke once defined decoration in terms of intentionality and arbitrariness.[13] For the generation of architects who began their careers in the postwar years, and particularly those who were educated at the Helsinki University of Technology in the 1950s, the thought of poetic construction was a means to purify their work of disorder and decoration. Their best works, like those of Blomstedt, are filled with an emptiness and a lucidity that has its source in deep meditations on a right-angled world. Few elements, much repetition, and a restrained palette of materials characterize the silent strength of the most significant works of this period.

In 1989 Aarno Ruusuvuori wrote, "When I was a young architect thirty years ago, the type of architecture I designed was based on the structural properties of concrete, and I have not yet had reason to abandon this principle."[14] Ruusuvuori, whose work has consistently been characterized by austere forms and a disciplined use of material and light, was a model of architectural toughness for the young Finnish architects who were studying at the University of Technology, where he taught during the same years as Aulis Blomstedt. His architecture at that time and to this day remains uncompromising and devoid of sentimentality. There is no narrative, no longing for another idyllic time, and no representational content. The hard edge of strict geometric forms creates a distinct boundary between his architecture and the natural aspect of things—a distance between civilization and the forest *(36)*. Yet in front of water or a boundless horizon he knows how to make architecture that aspires to breathe well *(37)*.

This world of form is unpretentious, straightforward, and unadorned. It achieves an unusual purity with the most minimal gestures. It is an architecture of repose in which line has the eternal immobility it once had in Egyptian art. In these lines there is an invitation to con-

36. *Aarno Ruusuvuori, Tapiola Church, Espoo, 1965*

37. *Aarno Ruusuvuori, sauna designed for industrial manufacture, commissioned by Marimekko, 1968*

template a world of pure form free from depiction, a world where architecture is emptied of everything inessential. But as modern as Ruusuvuori's purist architecture is in its abstract form, it has a quality of asceticism that establishes continuity with traditional Finnish architecture, where the use of a single material and the imprint of a tool were enough to create a lasting effect.

The Search for Elemental Presence

Asceticism as an artistic quality became synonymous with Finnish architecture and design in the 1950s. In the IX Milan Triennale held in 1951, Tapio Wirkkala alone won an unprecedented three Grand Prix, and he followed that success with an additional three Grand Prix at the 1954 Triennale. The strength of his work was based upon the most basic design principles. "There is an unwritten law that applies to all materials, which we tend to ignore. The designer should never do violence to the materials he is working on; rather he should seek harmony with them," Wirkkala wrote with candid simplicity.[15]

Minimal forms and the desire for the elegance of a primitive gesture are aspects of Wirkkala's designs that remain relevant in our time, not because of their newness or uniqueness but because of their contact with something inexhaustibly old.

His constructions with the pure geometric outline in glass rely on fundamental objective criteria—the circle, the square, and the triangle—and their ageless, absolute, and universal beauty *(38–40)*.

39. Tapio Wirkkala, blown glass, 1962

40. Tapio Wirkkala, geometric construction of glass, 1966

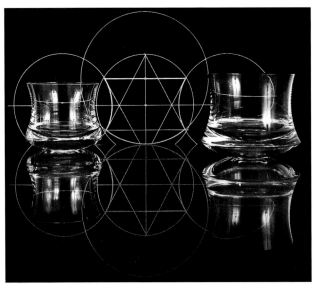

38. Tapio Wirkkala, glass based on constructivism and optic impression, 1956

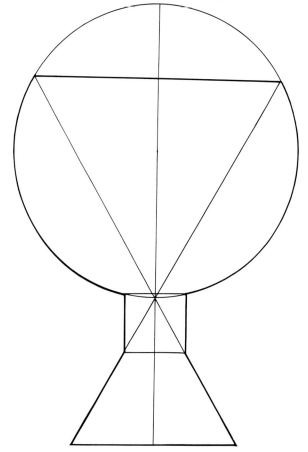

Kaj Franck's elemental forms in ceramic and glass have this same timeless presence, this same search for the essence of an object—a search for the sound of first words. The primitive quality that was found in Finnish handicrafts prior to the twentieth century survives in Franck's frugal objects. They are as anonymous as a peasant tradition, yet they are mass-produced and somehow survive what he called the "attack of industrialization."[16]

For Franck, industrial design was not a question of style, but a matter of essence. He was constantly searching for the means to create objects that were utterly authentic—that held the truth in the most plain and unassuming form. "A product does not age with changing fads; it is not bound to its own time alone but can live in unison with time,"[17] Franck said. His ability to create timeless forms makes his work as ageless today as the moment it came into being *(41)*.

Franck could make an object as fragile as an egg, but the durable objects that he created in glass and ceramics are the most lasting. It is as if there were a correlation between the physical weight of these objects and their ability to withstand time aesthetically. The heavy ones hold time like a stone in their eternally lucid lines. They are nameless and enduring. They almost disappear *(42)*.

The chapel designed by Heikki and Kaija Sirén at Otaniemi in 1957 *(43, 44)* captured in architectural form the clarity and elemental purity both Wirkkala and Franck achieved in their objects. In this small building everything but the essence has been taken away. Only three walls, two rooms, and the order of the square and its right angle have been left behind to give material radiance to light's invisible presence. In their singularity these walls hold nothing more than the silence of time, and in their stillness they stand as if they knew that nothing more was needed. In the late twentieth century, when excess so often leads to architectural poverty, it is reassuring to know that so much can be pared away.

Prefabricated Silence

In 1966, the year Robert Venturi wrote "less is a bore,"[18] young architects in Finland were constructing the foundations of their careers on the tradition of modernism, convinced that it was a vital force and that less, in fact, was more.

The thought of realizing architecture from the mass-produced and standardized parts made available by modern industrial society characterized the early works of many Finnish architects who completed their studies at the Helsinki University of Technology in the 1960s and early 1970s.

In retrospect, the great promise these architects saw in prefabrication seems naïve, but their vision went beyond thoughts of allying architecture with industrial production; their aim was to achieve a poetics of construction.

Apprenticeship to this rational school of restraint reinforced the notions of line, material limit, and proportional discipline which had been instilled in the young architects by their teachers and by the model of ordinary vernacular buildings that for centuries in Finland used the single material of wood and the length of a log as a module for beautiful utility.

For Kristian Gullichsen, Erkki Kairamo, Kirmo Mikkola, and Juhani Pallasmaa, who were among the leaders of the constructivist movement in Finland, prefabrication was a means to reconcile timeless architectural and artistic concerns with contemporary technology. Individually and in various forms of collaboration with one another they sought clear architectural concepts in the thought of construction.

Gestures of silence reverberate in the grid and the frame in the early architectural collaborations of Kirmo Mikkola and Juhani Pallasmaa. In their design for the Relander Residence in central Finland, the stillness of construction is poised against the immensity of nature. The breakdown of scale, the rhythmic pattern of the module, and the serenity of the horizontal line form a

41. *Kaj Franck, clear and gray glass pitchers, Nuutavärvi Glassworks, 1950s*

42. *Kaj Franck, ceramic pitchers, Arabia Ceramic Works, 1950s*

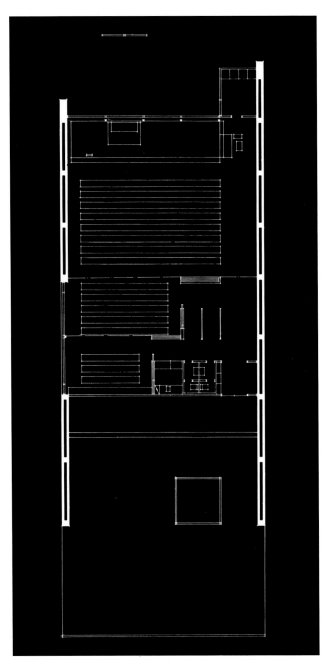

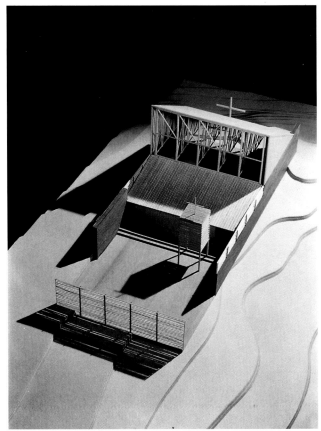

43. *Kaija and Heikki Sirén, model for the Otaniemi Chapel, Espoo, 1957*

44. *Kaija and Heikki Sirén, plan for the Otaniemi Chapel, Espoo, 1957*

harmonious contrast with the thin verticality of the birch forest and emphasize the calm mood evoked by this humble form *(45)*.

Every line seeks repose, and the tension of precise geometry resonates from the edge of the frame to the innermost room. The clarity of the plan and its austere and simple appearance recall traditional Finnish constructions in wood, but there is no sense of nostalgia. From the inward planes of enclosure to the lines of transparency at the edge of the frame, there is a continual

45. *Kirmo Mikkola and Juhani Pallasmaa, Villa Relander, Muurame, 1966*

46. *Kirmo Mikkola and Juhani Pallasmaa, Villa Relander, Muurame, 1966*

ceived that stupidity was not at all diminished by progress, but that stupidity in fact increased along with progress.[21]

By the late 1960s, when much of the speculative damage had already been done, a small group of architects was asked to work on standards for concrete prefabrication, but the effort was begun a generation too late to have a significant effect.[22] The California rationalist Pierre Koenig, an architect of Case Study Houses for *Arts + Architecture* in the 1950s, wrote that he did not expect good results from architects working with industry: "Industry has not learned the difference between what is beautiful in its simplicity and what is ugly although equally simple."[23] This problem, it seems, has only been exaggerated with increasing abundance.

Significant breakthroughs were made during this period by architects who had confidence in prefabrication and saw in its restrictions a means to achieve the ideals implied by constructivism. Like Aulis Blomstedt, they believed that the problem with standardization was not a function of increased flexibility but a matter of constructing systems that were non-elastic in the right way.

The Autonomy of the Grid

The calm of studied simplicity pervades the minimal form of the Moduli 225 system for prefabrication in wood *(47, 48)*, designed by Kristian Gullichsen and Juhani Pallasmaa. Classic proportions, precision of execution, and a denial of the superfluous clarify the structural order of their modular design. While the design is based on the repetition of a simple modular grid, the architectural significance of the work is less in the construction itself than in the contemplative realms that it suggests.

The idea that architecture could act as a social catalyst was an essential aspect of constructivist thinking in Finland. In this sense the idea of anonymous serial production in Gullichsen and Pallasmaa's design was a direct criticism of the personal indulgence that characterized expressionist tendencies in Finnish architecture. At the same time, their work maintains a critical distance from industrial production in that there is no sense of a fetish for the machine and little regard for early functionalist thinking that sought the form of a culture in works of the machine. One could even say that the details of their design exhibit a tectonic primitivism and a feeling of anonymity common to vernacular building, rather than an image evocative of the machine age.

The reconciliation of the machine and the spirit separates Gullichsen and Pallasmaa's architectural idea from the thoughts of an early constructivist such as László Moholy-Nagy, who wrote in 1922, "To be a user of machines is to be of the spirit of this century. It has replaced the transcendental spiritualism of past eras."[24] The resolution of what Moholy-Nagy saw as two opposing and irreconcilable forces is precisely what makes

interaction with the outside, and the presence of nature permeates the pure form of the house *(46)*.

The solitude of this house is its most striking characteristic. The exactitude of geometry and its edges of clarity create a spatial tension that intensifies the lonely presence of this house in the forest. It is stripped of decoration without remorse, and in its emptiness there is nothing left but the silence of construction.

Overabundance and Standardization

Alvar Aalto often used the term elastic standardization to describe his position in regard to industrial production. For Aalto, the idea of mass production was more than an economic issue. When he wrote that a "psychological slum"[19] was emerging from short-sighted industrial production methods, or later that "standardization involves industrialized violence against individual taste,"[20] it is clear that the subordination of the individual to the collective structure of society was at the center of his thoughts.

Without question, standardization driven by consumer materialism created an atmosphere for some of the worst architecture in Finland in the twentieth century. Aalto's most pessimistic predictions were realized. And, sadly, the most disheartening results occurred in the realm of housing. In the 1960s and 1970s the technical knowledge required to produce prefabricated elements grew far more rapidly than any wisdom regarding their use.

When one looks at these houses today, the realist Flaubert comes to mind. In his thought-provoking book *The Art of the Novel*, Milan Kundera wrote that Flaubert made one of the greatest discoveries of the nineteenth century: according to Kundera, Flaubert correctly per-

47. *Kristian Gullichsen and Juhani Pallasmaa, Moduli 225 system, 1970*

48. *Kristian Gullichsen and Juhani Pallasmaa, Moduli 225 system, 1970*

Gullichsen and Pallasmaa's design significant.

Juhani Pallasmaa has written, "A house may seem to be built for a practical purpose, but in fact it is a metaphysical instrument, a mythical tool with which we try to introduce a reflection of eternity into our momentary existence."[25] Although these words were written over ten years after he and Gullichsen completed the design of Moduli 225, one could already sense in this work the feeling of "metaphysical loneliness" that Pallasmaa would later see in the architectural motifs of Edward Hopper's paintings or in Walker Evans's photographs *(49)*.

Introducing an unconscious dimension of silence into the grid of industrial production gives this work by Gullichsen and Pallasmaa a rare potency. The structural rhythm of vertical and horizontal elements is unequivocal and precise, and in its candid, structural approach there is a sense of authenticity. It shares with Alvar Aalto's stool *(50)*, designed two generations earlier, an unaffected simplicity and a utopian desire for the humanization of technology. At the same time, its austere form questions the overwhelming multiformity made available by industrial production.

49. *Kristian Gullichsen and Juhani Pallasmaa, Moduli 225 system, Sauna, 1970*

50. *Alvar Aalto, Stool 60, birch, 1932–33*

51. *Kristian Gullichsen, La Petite Maison, Grasse, France, 1972*

52. *Erkki Kairamo, Liinasaarentie Multifamily House, Espoo, 1971*

"What really enriches an individual's life in a time such as ours?" the Japanese architect Tadao Ando has asked. "It is important to discover what is essential to human life and to consider what abundance truly means."[26] In its material configuration the Moduli 225 asks us to consider the question that Ando has put into words with such eloquent simplicity.

Paradoxical Anonymity

In the production of constructivist architecture, the anonymity of industrial technique and the restraints that it places upon the architect would seem to preclude personal expression. On the contrary, when one looks at the early works of Kristian Gullichsen, Erkki Kairamo, or Juhani Pallasmaa, the unmistakable identity of the individual architect is present in the architecture even though each one is striving for the universal.

It would be difficult to confuse the hard edge and restless lines of Kairamo's work with the calm absence of motion in Gullichsen's earth-bound horizontals *(51)*. Even when Kairamo's lines are enclosed in a rectangular frame, the tension of bound energy is relentless *(52)*. Mechanisms of motion, revealed in hardware that allows screens to slide or that are implicit in the exceptional diagonal of an exterior stair, only hint at Kairamo's desire to make the line move. The interiors of his Liinasaarentie houses resonate with lines of force seeking infinite horizontal and vertical extension *(53)*. The classic notion that walls could hold the energy of a room is shattered by layers of proportional geometry that dynamically project, overlap, and fold on one another. Everything is directed from the core outward, and everywhere the stillness is fractured. It is astonishing to think that all of this energy originates in a basic grid of load-bearing points and a simple supporting surface.

Erkki Kairamo's architecture shares with Juhani Pallasmaa's design for a two-family house in Helsinki basic neoplastic and constructivist elements of form. Both constructions are carefully proportioned, repetitive, and dependent to a large extent on prefabricated materials. They are hardly touched by the "impurity" of function, yet they function well. In each design an interior core is released at an outer edge by screens that deny the duality between outside and inside, and, in no uncertain terms, each of these works rejects the decorative line. While their ideas share a quality of precise execution and a simplicity of expressive means, the contrasts and oppositions embedded in Pallasmaa's work clearly separate his design from the dynamic force of Kairamo's steel construction. In Pallasmaa's design for the Enarvi duplex, plane and point, open and closed, hand-formed and preformed, depth and surface, wall and frame, and the protection of the inside and the exposure of the edge all form a unified whole based on number, proportion, and the plastic means of line and color *(54)*.

53. Erkki Kairamo, Liinasaarentie Multifamily House, Westend, Espoo, 1971

all, the weightless presence given definition by the taut skin and deep voids of the facade is denied by a concrete core that forms a distinct counterpoint to the lean exterior. As a model for industrial feasibility, the house employs factory-formed elements, but their expression is always subservient to the idea that a house is a product of the architect's imagination.

In the late 1930s, Piet Mondrian wrote that it was wrong to think that the nonfigurative artist creates through "the pure intention of his mechanical process," or that through "calculated abstractions" there was a "desire to suppress sentiment not only in himself but in the spectator." He says further:

That which is regarded as a system is nothing but constant obedience to the laws of the purely plastic, to necessity, which art demands from him [the artist]. It is thus clear that he has not become a mechanic, but that the progress of science, of technique, of machinery, of life as a whole, has only made him into a living machine, capable of realizing in a pure manner the essence of art. In this way, he is in his creation sufficiently neutral, that nothing of himself or outside him can prevent him from establishing that which is universal.[27]

Impulses from de Stijl and the California rationalists, whose Case Study Houses were influential in Finland in the 1960s, merge with a desire to bring artistic purpose to modern industrial culture. Following Piet Mondrian's law of the denaturalization of matter, Pallasmaa opposes the natural representation of things with the abstract purity of primary color in the Enarvi duplex. Panels of red, yellow, and green are organized in terms of constructive relations and stress fundamental laws specific to artistic culture.

The experimental quality of the house is further heightened by the use of glass, metal, and plastic. When a traditional material such as wood is employed, its original sensuous quality is purified by proportion, saturated by color, and made exact by industrial fabrication. Over-

It is precisely this desire for an impersonal art of restraint and discipline that gives the Enarvi house its formal power. Like much of the constructivist architecture realized in Finland from 1950 through the 1970s, it relies on an explicitly stated idea.

Reima Pietilä's description of the genesis of his design for the Malmi Church competition of 1967 provides a vivid contrast to constructivist thinking.

Our cat came to rest on the drawing board, and lay across the drawing before me. It visually terrorized me into accepting the form language of its own physiognomy for my free-sketch form. Missukka was a domestic Finnish cat— grey and striped transversally in a darker grey. Well, I said to her, I accept your shape because otherwise I can't make this competition. Then I drew a pencil line around the shape of the cat's body, fixing its configuration on my plan.[28]

54. Juhani Pallasmaa, Enarvi Duplex, Tammisalo, Helsinki, 1973

Such an acceptance of shape and chance was a world apart from the ideals of the constructivists, who saw the tradition of modern architecture as their inheritance, the union of art and industry as their social responsibility, and innovation their last resort. Their desire for purity and simplicity, and their denial of personal expression recall the early manifestos of the neoplasticists. "Our era is inimical to subjective speculation in art, science, technology and so on," wrote van Doesburg and van Eesteren in 1923. "The new spirit which already governs almost all modern life is opposed to animal spontaneity (lyricism), to the dominion of nature, to complicated hairstyles and elaborate cooking."[29]

The Art of Building

By the 1970s the collaboration (which had begun in the 1950s with the foundation of Group 4) between constructivists in the pictorial arts and architecture, and a Finnish section of the French organization L'Espace had expanded with the formation of the Dimensio Group, which included musicians, filmmakers, and sculptors in addition to painters and architects.

When one looks at the design of the wall and stair in Kirmo Mikkola's *Ateljeetalo* in Järvenpää, the purity of luminous geometry and a sense of spatial infinity bring painting to mind. The burden of use has almost disappeared in the lightness of the elegant lines. Without question this wall and stair are a material construction, but

55. *Kirmo Mikkola, Ateljeetalo Artists' Houses, Järvenpää, 1967*

the silent, inexplicable, and eternal aspects of their immateriality bring them close to pure form *(55)*.

Mikkola's design simultaneously appeals to the spirit and the intellect. On the one hand, the silence of the work calls upon what Mikkola referred to as the meditative need of man, and its transcendent form recalls the spiritual vibration of which Wassily Kandinsky once spoke. At the same time, modulations of number, geometric relations, and the subtle positioning and variance of line purify the form intellectually.

In this remote northern place where light struggles against dark, Mikkola's wall is a fragment of diaphanous silence—an elusive vision of a world of serenity. It is like the radiant silence that emanates from the face of a monk in a Tarkovsky film or the mystic calm of a saint in an orthodox icon *(56)*. It could make the noise of the world tremble.

The abstract form of Mikkola's design realizes the constructivist dream of dissolving the boundary between art and life. His wall and stair are part of a housing complex that participates in everyday life, but fragments of this construction emerge from a thought of harmony and a desire for the ideal; they belong solely to the world of the spirit.

This architecture recalls early modern painting and, in particular, the words of the suprematist Kazimir Malevich, who said, "My new painting does not belong solely to the earth. The earth has been abandoned like a house, it has been decimated. Indeed, man feels great yearning for space, a gravitation to break free from the globe of the earth."[30]

Mikkola's delicate lines form a spiritual vision of a world relieved of matter, a world close to the beginnings of geometry and the origin of pure light. But unlike suprematist form, it does not strive for a liberation from utility. It recognizes function. This wall and stair form an image that is perhaps the most profound realization of the constructivist interpretation of *Rakennustaide*, or building art—the Finnish word for architecture.

The Song of Geometry

Kirmo Mikkola's construction shares an aspiration to the condition of sonorous geometry with some of the most notable works in Finnish art, architecture, and industrial design. Paradoxically, these works that employ the most elementary geometric forms, that excise abundance, that call for restraint, and that demand the acceptance of tradition leave the most room for our imagination. One might even say that they force us into contemplation.

Like Mikkola's architecture, Raimo Utriainen's aluminum sculptures are machines for building the song of geometry. They may be constructed from metallic substances, but the slow flames of light that move through the form of their golden sections suggest immateriality and essence *(57)*.

Juhana Blomstedt achieves in his paintings *(58)* a

57. Raimo Utriainen, "Square in a square," polished anodized aluminum, 1982

similar distance from figuration through the sharp edge of precise, rectilinear geometry and the tension of lines. They create what he calls "a field of force"[31] on the surface of the canvas. What is remarkable in Blomstedt's painting and in so much of the artistic production of Finland's constructivists is the utter confidence in the mystical dimension of the straight line. Their use of this unchanging form provided a source of limitless possibility and endless contemplation. Even today the simple straight line remains beyond understanding and refers to nothing other than itself.

The sparse complexity and simple forms of constructivism have become accepted principles within the tradition of modernism in Finland. Since 1950 constructivism has been a thick wall of resistance to subjective expression, and in recent times, when historicism, figuration, and literary thinking became fashionable in architecture, Finland's rationalists continued to rely on the essence of the inexplicably old, the nonfigurative, and the poetic in their search for fundamental laws of art and universal beauty *(59)*.

Architecture and Spiritual Matter

The silence of constructivism is an alien thought to much of the modern world. Objects seem to have lost contact with silence. How is it that in an encounter with an object an interval of silence is almost unendurable? And why does modern man dread those moments of silence upon which the presence of a thing depends? In a world dominated by the restless substance of international civilization and the relentless words of the mass media, we have, in many ways, lost contact with the silence contained in an object. In the noise of the modern world things seem to be hidden. A thing can be so engulfed in the velocity of information that its presence can be forgotten—or, even worse, thought inessential.

The inauthenticity that surrounds modern man makes the authentic almost unrecognizable. It is little

59. Kaija and Heikki Sirén, Student Chapel, Otaniemi, 1957

41

56. *Nineteenth-century cenotaph of St. Sergius and St. Herman, founders of the Valamo Monastery on Lake Laatokka (now Lake Ladoga, USSR), in the collection of the Orthodox Church Museum, Finland*

58. Juhana Blomstedt, acrylic painting from the "Genesis" series, 1985

wonder that Kaj Franck remarked, "Nobody believes anymore that the world can be transformed by a beautiful everyday object."[32]

In regard to lost hope, Aarno Ruusuvuori has written:

In our era of industrial materialism, buildings are frequently considered as mere structures of utility and objects of investment without any spiritual task. Consequently, our daily environment is failing in its fundamental task of bringing meaning and hope to our lives.[33]

Longing for the ideal in a time that is increasingly driven by utility and pragmatism—one in which technology often becomes an end in itself—seems to be an almost hopeless task. But the moments of silence left behind by Finland's constructivists, minimalists, and purists communicate something of universal significance in a time when so many architects have forgotten the possibility of hope in their art. Amid the insignificance of so much of modern life, the utter authenticity of the most profound rationalist works in Finland suggest a future in the ideals of modernism. They remind us of the profound message that initiated the modern movement: "that dream of a better, more beautiful and more real world."[34]

NOTES

1. Alvar Aalto, "The RIBA Discourse: The Architect's Struggle," *Sketches*, 145.
2. Paul Valéry, preface to "Man and the Sea Shell," in *Paul Valéry: An Anthology* (Princeton: Princeton University Press, 1977), 111–112.
3. The Winter War between Finland and the Soviet Union began in the autumn of 1939 and ended with the Peace Treaty of Moscow on March 12, 1940. Finland retained her independence, but ceded territory along the Finnish-Russian border.

   Finland joined the larger European conflict as an ally of Germany in 1941, in part to regain territories lost to the Soviet Union in the Winter War and in part to avoid occupation by either side during the war. An armistice was negotiated on August 19, 1944.

   As a consequence of losing the war, Finland ceded additional territories to the Soviet Union and was required to pay enormous war debts. Repaying these war reparations caused a restructuring of Finland's economy.
4. In 1950, for example, two-thirds of Finns lived in rural districts. But by 1980 three-fourths of the Finnish population had moved to urban areas. In Vilhelm Helander and Simo Risto, *Suomalainen Rakennustaide* (Helsinki: Kirjayhtymä, 1987), 27.
5. Aulis Blomstedt, "Man the Measure of Architecture," *Arkkitehti* 2 (1971): 62.
6. Aulis Blomstedt, in exhibition catalogue *Studies in Harmony*, by Juhani Pallasmaa, trans. Leena Moorhouse and Jonathan Moorhouse (Helsinki: Museum of Finnish Architecture, 1980), 15.
7. Aulis Blomstedt, unpublished manuscript, eds. Kirmo Mikkola and Juhani Pallasmaa, No. 33.
8. Aulis Blomstedt, manuscript, No. 78.
9. Aulis Blomstedt, manuscript, No. 79.
10. Alvar Aalto, quoted in Kirmo Mikkola, "From the Technological to the Humane: Alvar Aalto versus Functionalism," *Abacus* 1 (Helsinki: Museum of Finnish Architecture, 1979), 137.
11. "Between 1957 and 1978 over a million new dwellings were built; this is two-thirds of the entire number of dwellings in the land at the end of the 1970s. Planning was obviously confronted with totally new demands and partly unforeseen problems." In Helander and Risto, *Suomalainen Rakennustaide*, 27.
12. Aulis Blomstedt, *Studies in Harmony*, 29.
13. Rainer Maria Rilke, *Letters on Cézanne*, ed. Clara Rilke, trans. Joel Agee (New York: Fromm International Publishing, 1985), 76.
14. Aarno Ruusuvuori, Foreword to *Concrete in Finnish Architecture*, ed. Jouni Kaipia (Helsinki: Museum of Finnish Architecture, 1989), 5.
15. Tapio Wirkkala, quoted in Juhani Pallasmaa, "The Arduous Art of Simplicity," *Form, Function, Finland* 3 (1985): 13.
16. Kaj Franck, "On Finnish Product Design," in *Muotoilijan Tunnustuksia* (Helsinki: Valtion painatuskeskus), 77.
17. Kaj Franck, quoted in Eeva Siltavuori, "A Dream of a Timeless Object," *Form, Function, Finland* 3 (1985): 42.
18. Robert Venturi, *Complexity and Contradiction in Architecture* (New York: The Museum of Modern Art, 1977), 17.
19. Alvar Aalto, "European reconstruction brings to the fore the most crucial problem facing architecture in our time," (1941) *Abacus* 3, ed. Asko Salokorpi and Maija Kärkkäinen, trans. Desmond O'Rourke (Helsinki: Museum of Finnish Architecture, 1982), 129.
20. Alvar Aalto, "Culture and Technology," (1947) *Sketches*, ed. Göran Schildt (Cambridge: MIT Press, 1979), 94.
21. "Hegel was convinced he had grasped the very spirit of universal history. But Flaubert discovered stupidity. I dare say that is the greatest discovery of a century so proud of its scientific thought. Of course, even before Flaubert, people knew stupidity existed, but they understood it somewhat differently: it was considered a simple absence of knowledge, a defect correctable by education. In Flaubert's novels, stupidity is an inseparable dimension of human existence. . . . But the most shocking, the most scandalous thing about Flaubert's vision of stupidity is this: Stupidity does not give way to science, technology, modernity, progress; on the contrary, it progresses right along with progress!"

    Milan Kundera, *The Art of the Novel*, trans. Linda Asher (New York: Grove Press, 1988), 162–163.
22. The study on concrete unit systems, begun in 1968, was developed by Kristian Gullichsen, Juhani Pallasmaa, and Matti Seppänen.
23. Pierre Koenig, quoted in Esther McCoy, *Case Study Houses 1945–1962* (Los Angeles: Henessy and Ingalls, 1977), 118.
24. László Moholy-Nagy, quoted in Frank Whitford, *Bauhaus* (New York: Thames and Hudson, 1984), 128.
25. Juhani Pallasmaa, "The Geometry of Feeling: A Look at the Phenomenology of Architecture," *Arkkitehti* 3 (1985): 99.
26. Tadao Ando, Introduction to *Tadao Ando*, ed. Kenneth Frampton (New York: Rizzoli, 1984), 24–25.
27. Piet Mondrian, "Pure Art and Pure Plastic Art" (1936), *The New Art—The New Life: The Collected Writings of Piet Mondrian*, ed. and trans. Harry Holtzman and Martin S. James (Boston: G. K. Hall and Co., 1986), 299.
28. Reima Pietilä, quoted in Malcolm Quantrill, *Reima Pietilä: Architecture, Context and Modernism* (New York: Rizzoli, 1985), 82.

29. Van Doesburg and van Eesteren, "Towards Collective Building," in *Programs and Manifestoes on 20th Century Architecture*, ed. Ulrich Conrads, trans. Michael Bullock (Cambridge: MIT Press, 1984), 67.

30. Kazimir Malevich, quoted in Demetri Sarabianov, "Kazimir Malevich and His Art," *Kazimir Malevich 1878–1935* (Amsterdam: Stedelijk Museum, 1988), 70.

31. Juhana Blomstedt, quoted in Ville Lukkarinen, "Point, Line and Plane—Juhana Blomstedt at the Border of Art" (Helsinki: Helsinki Art Hall Exhibition, 1989), 81.

32. Kaj Franck, quoted in Eeva Siltavuori, "A Dream of a Timeless Object," 44.

33. Aarno Ruusuvuori, Opening Remarks for the seminar "Genius Loci: A Search for Local Identity" (Helsinki: SAFA, 1982), 7.

34. Kaj Franck, quoted in Eeva Siltavuori, "A Dream of a Timeless Object," 44.

Aulis Blomstedt

The following excerpts are from writings, diary entries, and unpublished manuscripts of Aulis Blomstedt. They are included to give the reader an indication of his theoretical position.

Elegance can only be achieved through asceticism.
(Studies in Harmony)

Culture implies striving toward integrity, clarity and precision in all fields and in all expressions.
(Studies in Harmony)

Doubt everything that does not appear simple.
simplex sigillum veri
(The Future of Architecture)

It is said that art is a means for expressing one's temperament—to me architecture is a means of disciplining temperament.
(Studies in Harmony)

We have strong habits of thinking which tempt us to identify architectural form with plastic form, but it is a mistake.

Restraint is the privilege of the great.

Architecture is geometry adapted to gravity.
(Diary entry)

Is the right angle the octave phenomenon of the visual world?
(Diary entry)

I avoid contriving—only the natural can be great.

Architecture is the art of subordination.
(On Architecture)

Architecture is choice, and few are able to choose right. The attraction seems to be "L'architecture phantastique"—just this kind of architecture that requires the least fantasy.
(The Future of Architecture)

Harmony is not dependent on material. It has its own order and is fully autonomous. Even the material must obey its laws.
(Studies in Harmony)

Numbers are not size, they are forms.
(Studies in Harmony)

The architect lives and works in the world of relations, proportions and measures. The success and even failure of our work depends on how well we know this world of relations, measures and proportions.
(The Architect's Position in Modern Society)

For me the concept classical does not mean a certain kind of style or 'age,' but in my opinion the word classical could be replaced with the word complete-tension.
(My Aims in Architecture)

In the clash of cultures, invariants are essential.
(Diary entry)

The basic element in architecture is the supporting surface.
(Diary entry)

Perhaps it seems too obvious or abstract when I state that horizontal and vertical lines together form the most general, basic fundamentals in architecture. Anyone who completely masters and understands them, masters almost all of architecture.
(The Alphabet of Architecture)

Every truly powerful period in architecture brings the core back to the surface.
(Prospects in Architecture)

If you want to create something new search for that which is ancient.

Architecture needs the existence of something old and timeless, like the cycle of the years, the rhythm of the moon, the majesty of the streams, or the old moss-covered rock.
(Studies in Harmony)

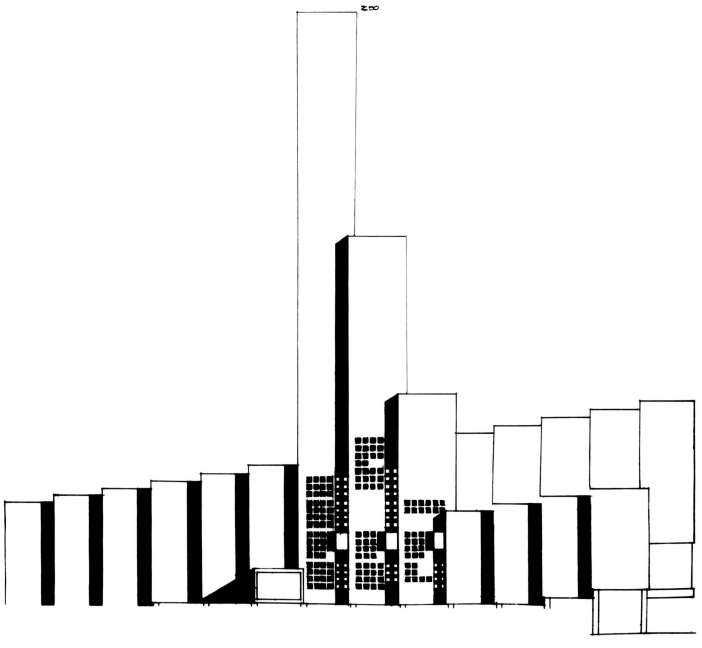

60. Aulis Blomstedt, Oslo Concert Hall project, 1957

47

61. Aulis Blomstedt, geometric design based on a square and even divisions of the number sixty

62. Aulis Blomstedt and Heikki Koskelo, Exhibition "Arkitektur i Finland," Stockholm

Kristian Gullichsen and Juhani Pallasmaa, construction detail, Moduli 225 system, 1970

ARCHITECTS

AARNO RUUSUVUORI

Bonsdorff Sauna • Kellosalmi, Padasjoki • 1985

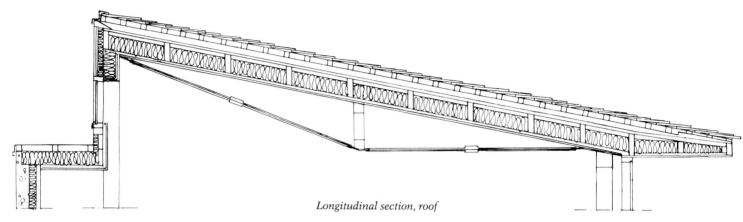

Longitudinal section, roof

Clarity of form and considered restraint have been characteristics of Aarno Ruusuvuori's architecture since he began building in the late 1950s. His constructions then as now depend upon minimal gestures and a limited palette of materials.

Built for the industrialist Veikko Bonsdorff on a north bank of Lake Päijänne in central Finland, the sauna is a small building with a huge presence. Cast concrete, pine, and stainless steel are the materials out of which the building is formed, but it is the component of silence that is the most active force in the building.

On the subject of silence, the

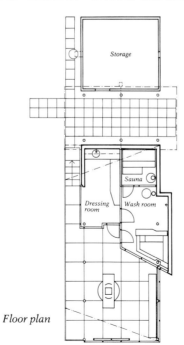

Floor plan

philosopher Max Picard has written, "In a world of silence a thing offers its being to man directly; it stands immediately before him as though it had just been brought by a special act out of the silence. It stands out clearly against the background of silence. There is no need to add anything to make it clear."

National Museum Extension • Helsinki • 1995

In the west courtyard of the National Museum (Herman Gesellius, Armas Lindgren, and Eliel Saarinen, 1902–10) Aarno Ruusuvuori deviated from the town plan by placing the new facilities underground.

Typical of Ruusuvuori's work, the architectural conception is without ambiguity. Basic geometries—the circle, the square, and the triangle—give order to the interior and suggest a world of form that is apprehensible by reason. The museum extension begins with geometry and light. At the junction of the existing museum and the new extension, the arc of a circle defines a light hall that physically joins the two buildings. But they are absolutely separate. Intellectually, Ruusuvuori's addition belongs to the rationalist school, and its position adjacent to a monument of Finnish National Romanticism revives an architectural dialogue nearly a century old.

Opposing the variety of materials, textures, and eclectic medieval motifs that dominate the existing museum, Ruusuvuori's extension relies on the singularity of reinforced concrete, minimal differentiation in texture, and a clear, formal statement based on modern architectural principles. The museum extension, like many of Ruusuvuori's earlier projects, reflects his career-long interest in the structural and aesthetic possibilities of reinforced concrete. And, as with these earlier works, there is a quality of asceticism that dominates the architectural expression.

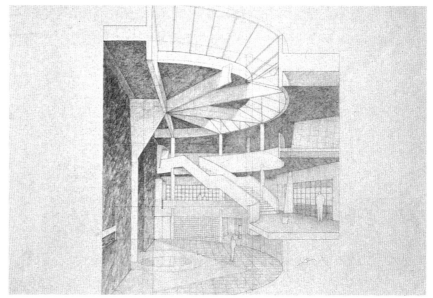

Section

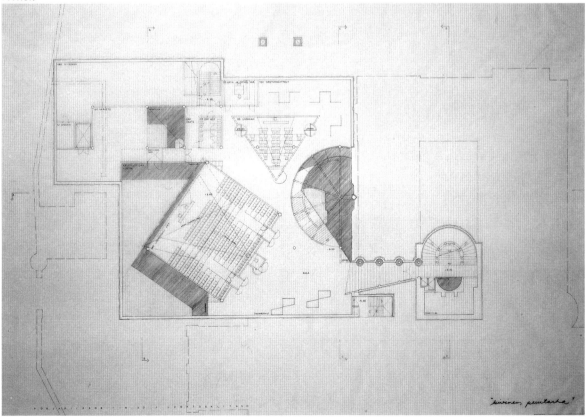

Plan

City Hall Restoration and Extension • Helsinki • 1965–88

When the first stage of the city hall-block renovation was completed in 1970, Aarno Ruusuvuori's radical juxtaposition of the new with the old was highly criticized. At that time the trend was toward conserving old buildings with minimal intervention on the part of the architect and Ruusuvuori's work was clearly counter to that trend.

The three-story building which faces the harbor and is now the main entry to the city hall was originally planned as the Seurahuone Club in 1833 by the architect Carl Ludvig Engel. Sixty-eight years later, the city purchased the building, but it was not until 1913 that a competition was arranged to transform the present city hall block into the new city hall. None of the competition entries were realized, however, and the Seurahuone Building became the new city hall without significant renovation.

Ruusuvuori's 1970 design transformed the building behind Engel's neoclassical façade with completely modern facilities. The minimalism and austerity of the interior architecture contrasts vividly with the profuse ornamentation that once adorned the interior rooms of the Seurahuone Building, but the plainness of the 1970 interior renovation is not an autonomous architectural expression—it is instead a reformation of aspects that are essential to the art of building in Finland. In

this respect, Ruusuvuori builds upon a tradition of simplicity, austerity, and silence.

The planning principles used in the first stage of renovation proved to be adaptable to later planning, and over time the project became a model for the rehabilitation of old buildings even outside of Finland. When a second extension was planned in the mid-1980s, Ruusuvuori used the same design framework to plan the new administrative core embedded in the middle of the block. An open plan based on a structure of columns, the use of a skylight to define the edge of a room, low horizontal lines making pockets of dark that accentuate the light, crisp lines, and precise detailing are common to both the 1970 renovation and the 1988 extension.

It should be noted that in addition to the renovation and extension, a row of eighteenth- and nineteenth-century buildings on Aleksanterinkatu, facing the cathedral, as well as buildings within the courtyard, were carefully preserved and restored. But it is the thoughtful opposition of the old and the new that gives this project its refined architectural quality. And, like a fine work of art, Ruusuvuori's rehabilitation of the city hall block becomes only better with the passing of time.

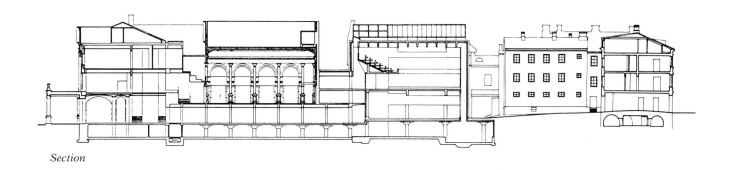

Section

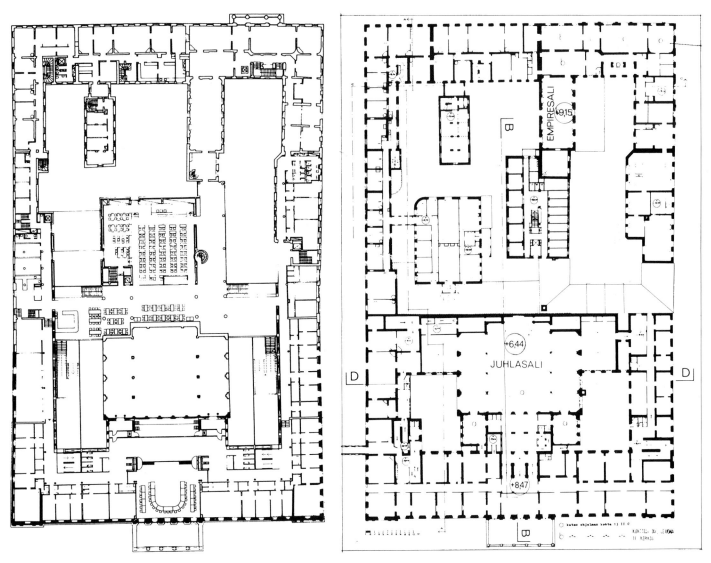

First floor plan

First floor plan before renovation

ARKKITEHDIT KY · GULLICHSEN-KAIRAMO-VORMALA

Parish Center · Kauniainen · 1983

Kristian Gullichsen's preference for an architecture of walls is apparent even in his earliest works. The small house he designed for his mother in the stepped terraces of an olive grove in southern France is ordered by a horizontal repetition of low walls and their power to control a site. On a larger scale, the walls of the Kauniainen Parish Center are barriers that protect and isolate an interior realm of contemplation.

Above the long western wall a single, uninterrupted roofline over sixty meters long contains curved forms and openings that animate the white stucco wall and suggest an inward, internal

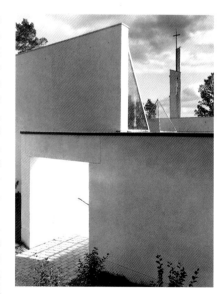

world. Along the wall, a sloping, stepped path joins the housing at the upper edge of the site with a commercial district and train station at its lower boundary. Beginning at the western boundary of the site, a low stone wall, reminiscent of those that mark the outermost boundary of Finland's medieval churches, delineates a path that leads to the main entry, which is located midway in the long wall.

At both ends of the building, walls separate it from the housing and commercial districts approached by the path. Against the northern border of the site, a singular white wall rises above

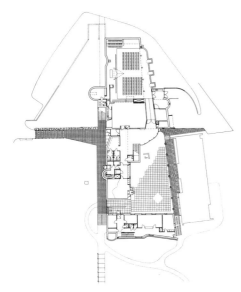

First floor plan

the main volume, rejecting everything but light for its inner side, while an undulating brick wall at the southern end of the site provides closure for an inner courtyard and a plane of resistance against profane life.

Built around an existing parish hall and church tower de-signed by the late Keijo Petäjä in 1964, the new parish center accommodates the older building as unselfconsciously as it assimilates influences ranging from modern masters to archaic sources to Finnish vernacular building customs.

The sequence that leads from the street at the western boundary of the site to the sanctuary—gate, path, immense wall, heavy door, dark path, light room—reveals a basic structure of Finnish architecture: an order based on the clarity of events. A border marked by a fence, a courtyard, a porch, a small room that changes the direction of movement, and an innermost room divided by light at the ground and dark above the rafters describes the distinct articulation of architectural events in a prevalent type of Finnish farmhouse; this clarity of events is also apparent in some of Alvar Aalto's most significant works, such as the Paimio Sanatorium, the Villa Mairea, and the Säynätsalo Town Hall. Gullichsen was raised from the age of seven in the Villa Mairea, and as a young architect he was an assistant in Aalto's office, so it is hardly unusual that he should adopt such a structure in his work.

Rather than step the building with the site, Gullichsen dug the church hall into the hillside, giving the subterranean path that leads to the sanctuary the impression of a dark and cold catacomb. From the main entry to the sanctuary Gullichsen employs changes in scale and light to close and open volumes in both the plan and section. Like Aalto before him, Gullichsen draws light from diverse sources, each giving a particular character to a room, a part of a room, or a passage between rooms. The illumination of the sanctuary, which begins with a series of light wells and a dark passage, is terminated in the church hall by a breach between the end wall and roof that allows southern light to flood over the choir. With the exception of several small openings punched in the wall, virtually all the light comes from the roof, giving the white austerity of the sanctuary an even radiance.

Inside the parish center, events are frequently layered, while in other places, such as the entry gate, they stand alone. The simultaneous freedom and dependency of events can be seen in the sanctuary, where the pulpit, altar, and baptismal font are designed as solitary objects that are nevertheless bound to the number three and the fact that three are one in the religious iconography of the Evangelical Lutheran Church.

Gullichsen's design is complex and clearly indebted to many sources, but the architecture is fresh. Gullichsen repays his debt by sustaining the liveliest aspects of tradition.

Longitudinal section

Stockmann Department Store Extension • Helsinki • 1989

Recent urban interventions in the center of Helsinki are as rare as they are conservative. There are few building sites, and speculation combined with a lack of architectural conviction led to banal buildings in the city center throughout the 1970s and early 1980s. Gullichsen, Kairamo, and Vormala's artistically ambitious project for one of Helsinki's most important corners is a stunning exception to this trend.

The site was difficult for a number of reasons. The new construction had to fit between John Settegren's eclectic hundred-year-old Argos Building and one of the most architecturally interesting buildings in Helsinki center, the original Stockmann Building, a somber ncoclassical design completed in 1930 by the architect Sigurd Frosterus. The building had to respond to the corner at both the roofline and the ground, at the junction of two of Helsinki's most important streets—Pohjoisesplanadi and Keskuskatu. And the long elevation on the Keskuskatu side faced two buildings designed by Alvar Aalto from 1955 and 1969 and another designed by Eliel Saarinen in 1920, while the short, southern façade fronted Jarl Eklund's curvilinear Swedish Theater whose exterior had been remodeled in 1936 by Eero Saarinen.

From the beginning of his career in the 1910s until 1956, Frosterus worked on plans that would have extended his original building over the entire block. Alvar Aalto also designed several unbuilt projects for the extension of Stockmann in 1961 and 1966, and he, like Frosterus, proposed the destruction of the Argos Build-ing. Interestingly, when the first stage of the competition was judged in 1984, very few of the competitors who chose to demolish the nineteenth-century building were considered to be among the top entrants, and all six competitors chosen for the second-stage competition preserved the eclectic building in their original entries.

The controversial Argos Building was ultimately saved, but in the final design its interior rooms were removed, leaving only a highly ornamented façade on the street. The wisdom of this partial preservation was a matter of debate at the time of the competition and remains so today, particularly in an era when we are just beginning to realize how many buildings with negligible qualities were "saved" from architecture in the past generation.

The constraints of the site, the conservation issue, and the intimidating presence of the Finnish masters on the adjacent streets seem to have raised the quality of the new architecture, which was a rare collaboration between all of the partners in the Arkkitehdit office. One exceptional quality of the building is the subtle way in which the architects express the relative artistic merits of the two existing buildings in the new addition. On the long Keskuskatu façade, the elegantly simple composition of glass and steel defers to the serenity of Frosterus's neoclassical landmark in such a manner that it appears as if the older, heavy building has almost transformed itself. There is absolute respect for the proportion and scale of Frosterus's architecture, yet there is no question that the

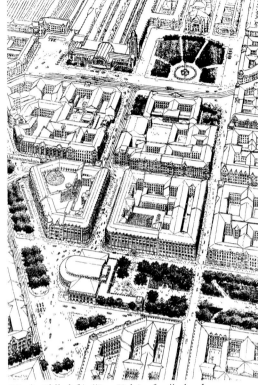

Site (middle left), "Pro Helsingfors" plan by Eliel Saarinen, 1920

artistic approach is utterly modern. Looking at the heavy masonry of the existing building against the new, crystalline façade, one might recall the poet Paul Scheerbart's intoxicating visions of a new glass culture and his 1914 statement: "We feel sorry for the brick culture."

By way of contrast, the Esplanadi elevation severs itself from the Argos Building with a thin wall that cuts like a knife as it rises to the sky. On the Esplanadi façade, architectural energies are

New extension, view toward Mannerheimintie (proposal by Alvar Aalto, 1955)

Original store, view toward Aleksanterinkatu, Sigurd Frosterus, 1930

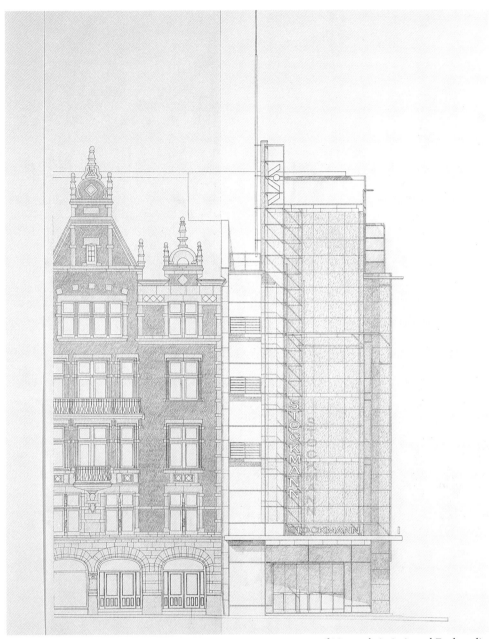

Argos Building, new addition (preliminary scheme) at intersection of Mannerheimintie and Esplanadi

focused more on making a corner than on establishing a dialogue with the older building. The low, sweeping curve of the entrance canopy protects the opening, controls the street, and, combined with a column, emphasizes the corner. Above the canopy a single balcony steps out of the façade, suggesting the possibility of public appearance. Although such an event rarely occurs, the balcony nevertheless allows the building to participate in the public realm above the ground, and, from the exterior, to engage an individual's imagination. In a restrained way, the isolated balcony recalls the image of dynamic movement formed by El Lissitzky's drawing of the Lenin Tribune—certainly a more important gesture than creating a dialogue with the Argos Building's balconies.

A most unfortunate circumstance in the Stockmann extension occurred inside the building: four different interior design firms did their best to ignore the fine architecture, an indication that Finnish architects have not yet fully regained the status they had lost in the past generation. Fortunately, however, interior fashion had no effect on how well the architects built the street.

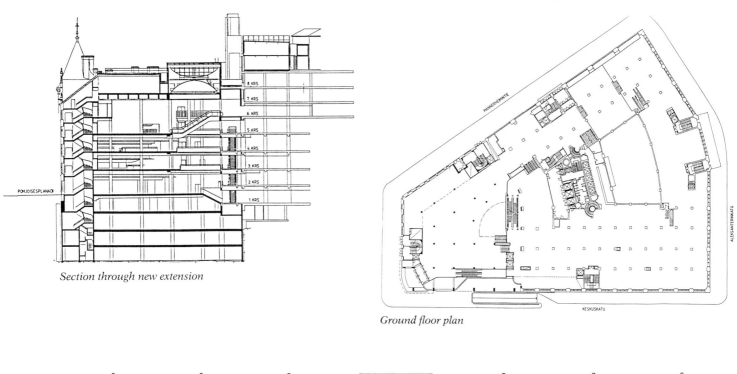

Section through new extension

Ground floor plan

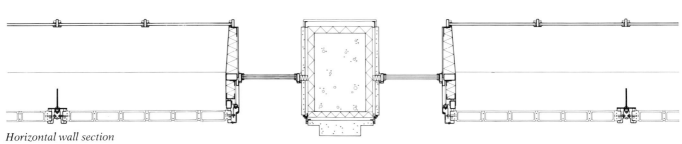

Horizontal wall section

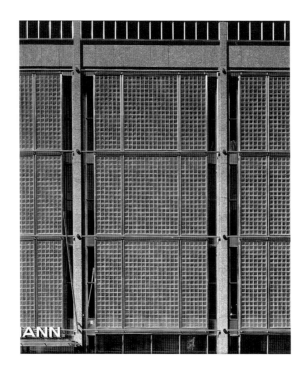

Cultural Center • Pieksämäki • 1989

As he did earlier in the Kauniainen Parish Center, Kristian Gullichsen uses walls to build the site and contain events. On the street side a row of trees, a linear forecourt, and a long, closed wall define an edge that controls the street and create a civic image on the scale of the town. But on the park side an equally long wall cuts into the sky and opens the inside to the trees and water. This wall, which accommodates a wider range of scales, suggests a domestic image in certain places and recalls the building's position as a center for a small community.

For Gullichsen, function does not determine form. His belief in the mutual independence of form and function allows him to explore the plastic quality of the wall in a manner free from the constraints of the parish center's multipurpose interior. Inside the walls, the primary functions—library, theater, exhibition area, and café—serve utilitarian purposes only partially indicated by changes in volume that occur on the exterior.

At times the relationship between the exterior and interior is straightforward and uncomplicated, particularly in the sitting room and its fireplace, the roof of the theater, the children's reading

room, and along the entire length of the west wall, where solids and voids articulate separate functions. But the walls of the cultural center can also be vague and offer no suggestion of the interior's contents. The long eastern wall, for instance, is a filter for light and view that makes an indeterminate boundary with the exterior and unifies rather than separates interior conditions.

The dramatic use of the stair, both as an opportunity to bring light into the building and as a stage for an individual's public appearance, recalls aspects of Aalto's architecture. Gullichsen shares Aalto's mannerist tendencies and his ability to control modest and monumental scales simultaneously. In all of Finnish architecture there is perhaps no greater shift in scale than the sequence that begins with the Roman grandeur of the Pieksämäki Cultural Center's portal and ends, only moments later, at the hearth of its cozy sitting room.

The optimism, certainty,

and purity implied by 1930s white, cubic functionalism is revived in the white stucco walls of the Pieksämäki Cultural Center. The walls recall a time when Finland's identity as a young, independent nation was bound to this positive image representing faith in the future. In his essay "The Architect's Conception of Paradise," Alvar Aalto wrote, "Architecture is the cheapest game. It is a game that, if we disregard the major religious epochs, most closely strives to realize a true humanism in our world, to create the very limited happiness one can offer man." It is astonishing to think that a building such as the Pieksämäki Cultural Center could be built by a community of less than fifteen thousand people. But even small Finnish communities realize the significance of architecture and the notion of cultural investment. This understanding has less to do with Finland's sudden affluence than it does with a cultural tradition. After all, one of the most highly regarded buildings of the twentieth century, Aalto's town hall in Säynätsalo, was designed for a community of three thousand inhabitants, who chose the internationally distinguished architect only after he submitted to a limited competition.

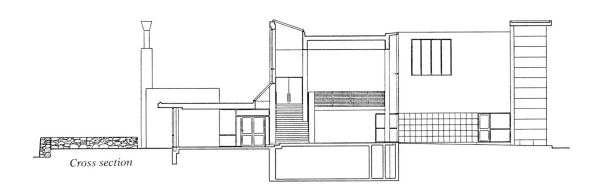

Cross section

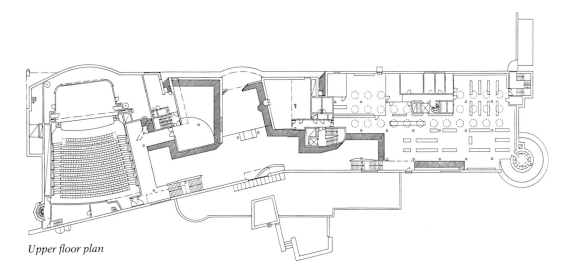

Upper floor plan

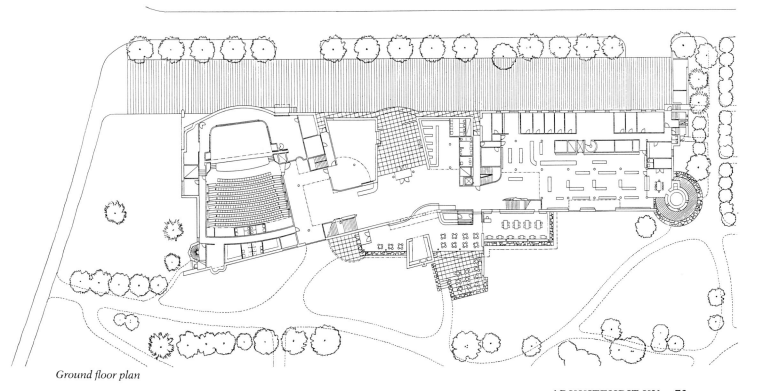

Ground floor plan

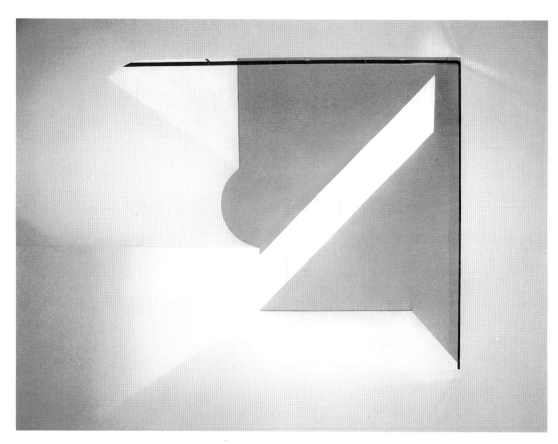

Four Residential Projects • Westend, Espoo

Liinasaarentie Multi-Family House, 1971

Liinasaarenkuja 3–5 Semidetached Houses, 1980

Hiiralankaari Apartment Block, 1983

Lyökkiniemi 6 Semidetached Houses, 1990

The Westend suburb of Espoo, located several kilometers from Helsinki center, has been an experimental laboratory for Erkki Kairamo's residential architecture for the past twenty years. Unlike his Liinasaarentie houses from the early 1970s, in which a classically static exterior contains the interior's vigorous lines, his most recent houses employ the movement of diagonals, spirals, and straight lines to bring this same dynamic quality to the exterior.

Over half a century separates Kairamo's most recent houses from the cubic functionalism of the 1930s, but the clarity, purity, and light implied by white modernism are still alive in his work. The monotony of "element construction" is brought into the realm of architecture by using the prefabricated core structure as a counterpoint to a secondary structure of individually formed parts. In this way, Kairamo uses the constraints of legal requirements (fire escape, stairs, and ladders) as well as balconies and terraces to make subtle adjustments in scale and to suggest the possibility of dwelling. These works are practical applications of the ideal of flexible standardization that Aalto spoke of half a century ago.

Both the Liinasaarenkuja semidetached houses and the Hiiralankaari apartment block are constructed from a basic core of prefabricated panels enhanced by elements that are structurally independent. The group of semidetached houses employs painted steel balconies, railings, and fences to give a vibrant image to the otherwise plain, economical, and structurally simple buildings that Kairamo describes as a "houses of cards." The nearby apartment block employs a similar principle, but in this case in situ concrete balconies are supported by the rigid frame.

Erkki Kairamo's initial residential project in Westend is separated from his semidetached houses at Lyökkiniemi 6 by a short walk, but they are joined by twenty years of searching along the same narrow architectural path. Clarity and simplicity in the architectural concept and an absolute faith in the artistic potential of the line have remained primary concerns. This architecture is as resolute as the wall that symmetrically divides the house.

Of all Kairamo's houses, Lyökkiniemi 6 most completely resolves the notion of interior and exterior as a single spatial entity.

In the winter, the horizontal line of trees in the distance, the white-blue planes of flat sky and frozen sea, and the single vertical lines formed by the birch trees in the foreground seem virtually to penetrate the house, only to be cultivated by geometry and proportional rhythm.

Unlike his houses from the 1980s, in which the dynamic quality emerged solely from elements applied to the core, the core of Lyökkiniemi 6 resembles the exterior. Everywhere the dynamic lines of force look for the sea—inside and out.

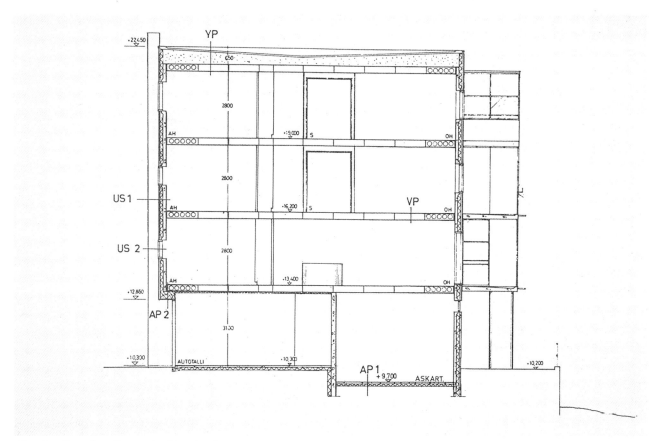

Cross section of continuous load-bearing frame

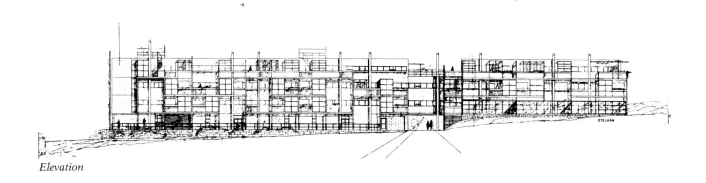

Elevation

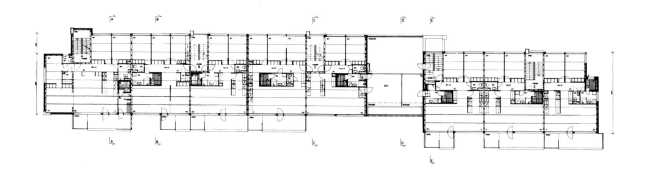

Second floor plan

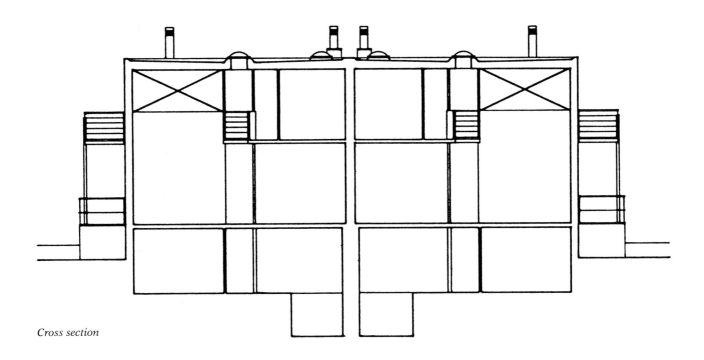

Cross section

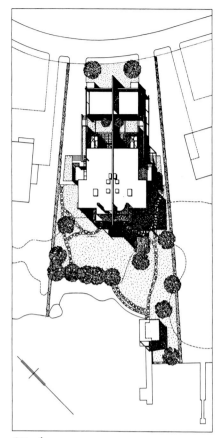

Site plan

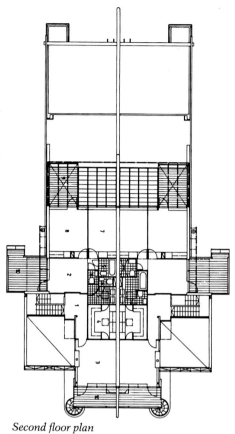

Second floor plan

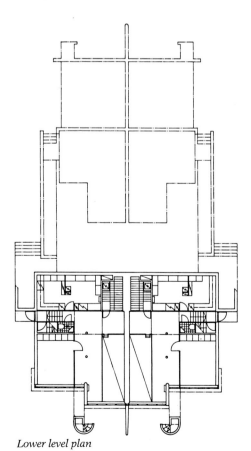

Lower level plan

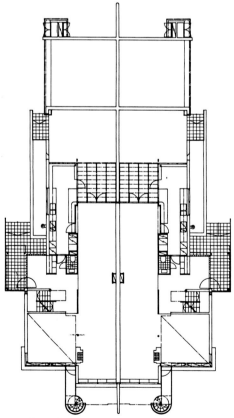

First floor plan

Itäkeskus Tower and Commercial Center • Helsinki • 1987

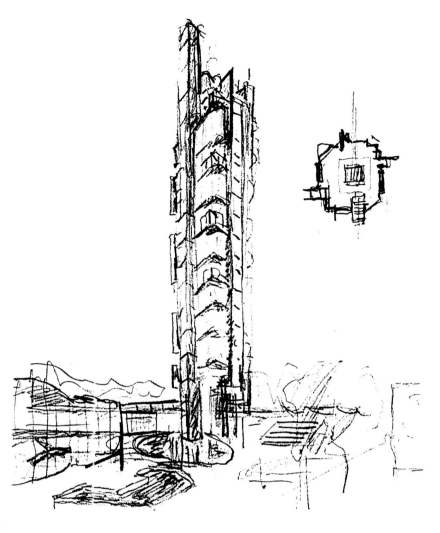

In the late 1970s several young architects asked Erkki Kairamo why he didn't change his style. His reply was simply: "I don't need to." Kairamo was not bragging. His words, like his work, are direct and clear. They express his conviction that architecture is renewed by tradition, in his case, the tradition of modernism. Kairamo has said, "Something new can only be a continuation of what is really valuable in the past."

The modernist tradition for Kairamo was not limited to architecture but had its roots in other art forms as well. He cites Eisenstein, Vigo, and Rossellini as primary influences. He says that the cinema was the source of his best architectural lessons.

Valomerkki (light signal), Kairamo's winning entry for a landmark tower in the East 1 Center suburb of Helsinki, uses repetition, isolated detail, and a cutting, insistent rhythm to give the sixteen-story tower a distinctive form. These same terms might be used equally well to describe images found in the unedited takes of Sergei Eisenstein's film ¡Que Viva Mexico!. Kairamo's use of repetition and rhythm to highlight the exceptional diagonal at the tower's roof is one example of the similarities between him and this master of the cinema. Clearly, another lesson drawn from the great directors is the ability to edit well.

Influences from early modern architecture are also apparent in Kairamo's design for the tower and commercial center—the Vesnin brothers' Pravda Tower and the diaphanous buildings of Gunnar Asplund's 1930 Stockholm Exhibition are the most obvious antecedents. Kairamo has strictly defined the limits of his architecture over the past twenty years, enabling him to assimilate modernist influences into his lyrical constructivism and make them his own.

It was Kairamo's intention that at night the new center's tower and commercial complex would be seen from the nearby highway as a suprematist cross-composition, with the lighted stairway of the tower as the vertical component for the horizontal lantern made by the length of the shopping center's illuminated glazing. During the day, when the cross of light is gone, the tower becomes less dynamic, remaining indifferent to all the horizontal motion and urban sprawl that surround it.

At every chance the vertical is emphasized in the tower. Ventilation ducts placed outside the building, a repetitive triangular section of floor that foreshortens as it rises, and the thrust of an eighty-two-meter-high stairway accentuate the slenderness of the tower, giving it the impression of being a much taller building.

As a focal point for this new suburb of thirty thousand people, the tower serves a primary architectural purpose that is more important than either commerce or the idolization of technique. As Kairamo himself said, "I consider my work a homage to man."

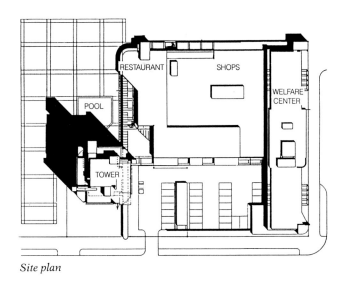

Site plan

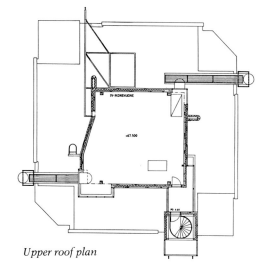

Upper roof plan

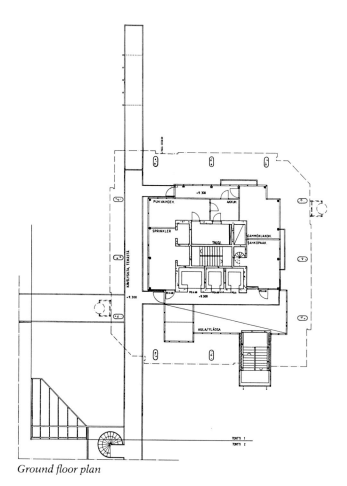

Ground floor plan

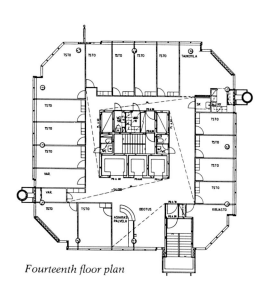

Fourteenth floor plan

JUHANI PALLASMAA

Art Museum • Rovaniemi • 1986

To collect and hold precious contents well requires a container and a seductive passage. Destinies have been determined by opening an irresistible box.

Juhani Pallasmaa's Rovaniemi Art Museum begins with the significance of entering. For Pallasmaa, entering is a primary architectural experience fraught with memory and feeling. Understatement and opposition deepen the experience. The immobility of a column against a passing cloud, a glass vestibule that is transparent yet impenetrable, and a door that allows entry but hides like a mask stimulates the imagination and prepares for a change in the view.

From a distance the entry is so inconspicuous that it almost disappears. But objects are positioned close to the threshold to challenge and accept everyday conditions. Five granite columns, two brass doors, and a glass vestibule separate center, and isolate the museum's threshold from the street. At this point the original brick building oscillates between being hardly altered and being radically transformed.

The granite, glass, and brass concentrated at the entry are enough to give the building its civic image, but scarcely call attention to that fact. Instead, the sensuousness of these materials—swirls of sediment, crystalline purity and hardness, layers of patina—call attention to their materiality. They recall a history of grandeur.

Sensuous material combined with archetypal form awaken the imagination and add a metaphysical dimension to the everyday experience of opening and entering. The door's archaic image is unfamiliar yet recognizable.

A door is an instrument of mystery, but when it becomes a mask it suggests a secret. And, like a mask, the museum's brass door hides and protects. It changes the

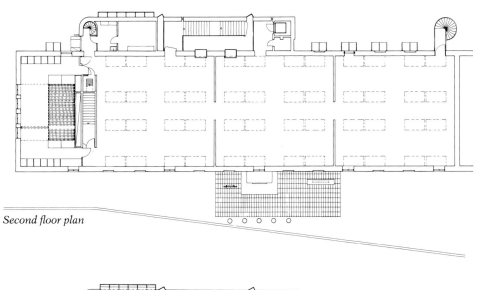

Second floor plan

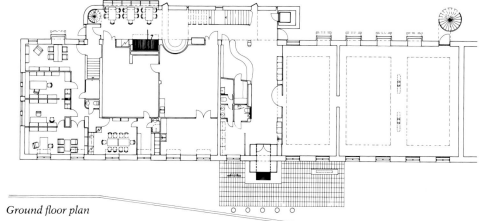

Ground floor plan

Site plan

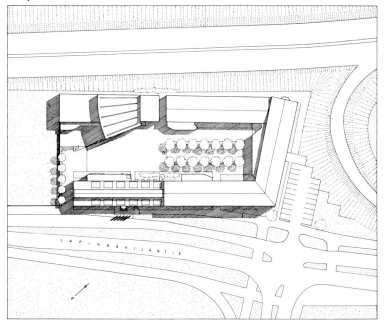

building and transforms the viewer. Between the mask and the museum there is a chance to recollect oneself, a compelling opportunity to forget deliberate action and to rely on spontaneous reaction. Crossing this boundary between outside and inside is as much an introspective act as it is a physical experience. Pallasmaa prepares the viewer to be alone. He believes that "experiencing art is a private dialogue between the work and the person experiencing it which excludes all other interaction." To step inside is to encounter solitude.

The interior galleries are a refuge from the street and a release from anticipation. Their plainness is sudden, even startling. Full of light, white paint, and plaster, these simple, functional rooms with their horizontal planes of blond wood exude a sense of warmth and calm. In their purity and simplicity they are close to the American Shaker rooms that Pallasmaa admires.

Between the first- and second-floor galleries, an annex to the original building holding a stair of granite, bronze, and steel disrupts the image of studied calm. But the discontinuity is purposeful. One must leave the original building and enter it again, underscoring the ambiguity of an exterior that has become an interior.

Breaking the dominance of a single mind is a characteristic of collage that Pallasmaa uses to create a composite presence rather than a singular image. Even before the renovation, Pallasmaa noted that the building was a collage of prewar Rovaniemi houses, since it was from these that the building was reconstructed after the wartime destruction of the town.

Pallasmaa's collage is a se-

quence of virtual entrances through layers of imagery. In this sequence of events continuity is subtly cut by an almost unnoticeable measure of silence that prepares the viewer to encounter the next image. Layers are assembled in such a way that each entity and each encounter flow into one another and are drawn into a unity.

The play of materials, texture, and time common to the method of collage is essential to Pallasmaa work. The successive moments that make the events

whole depend upon remembering. The fragility of the glass vestibule, for example, is heightened by the solidity of granite, even when these stone cylinders can no longer be seen. As one passes the brick wall and enters, the cylinders become a memory and as such anticipate the next material change inside.

With clarity and precision, Pallasmaa balances structure and event. He makes a room for each material and creates a distance between each texture. Even when they are juxtaposed, materials retain their individual presence, yet participate in the invisible form of the whole.

Jiři Kolař, a Czech artist whose work Pallasmaa admires, said, "The world attacks us directly, tears us apart through the experiencing of the most incredible events, and reassembles us again. Collage is the most appropriate medium for illustrating this reality."

In a world consumed by chronological time, Pallasmaa helps us to differentiate between the time of the clock and the time of the imagination. He helps us to see with fresh eyes.

Cross section

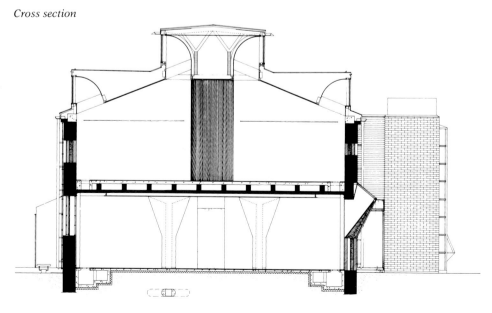

Institut Finlandais (Finnish Institute) • *Paris* • *1991*

Juhani Pallasmaa with Roland Schweitzer and Sami Tabet (Collaborator), Paris

The Finnish Institute is located between the Sorbonne and the historic Cluny Abbey which contains Roman ruins. The institute occupies two floors and a basement in a stone building built in 1862. Previous to its current use, the building had been occupied by the Cinéma Cluny, which was particularly popular among the students of the Sorbonne.

The severe, modern image of the Finnish Institute heightens the existing Parisian ambiance through considered opposition. A conscious balance, based on tension, has been formed between the old and the new; it emphasizes the thought, initialized by Adolf Loos, that a total absence of ornament is the appropriate image of the modern city. At the street, the only intervention is a modular glass-and-steel facade that projects slightly from the existing mid-nineteenth-century building. Its modern expression is intensified by the eclectic array of restless details that surround it. Pediments of varying heights and configurations, ornamental keystones, and a Renaissance portico create a visual image of variety and movement that opposes the

new façade's minimal gesture of absolute immobility.

Inside the building, however, the rigor and discipline of the exterior image are softened by the tactility of the interior rooms. The deliberate juxtaposition of modular principles with sensual content heightens one's awareness through utter contrast. This startling combination gives the door exaggerated importance as the means of separating two worlds—outer and inner.

Much of Pallasmaa's recent architecture revolves around the theme of the door. It reflects his preoccupation with the knowledge of being. For Pallasmaa, to make a door means to question its nature. The front door of the institute, a solid plate of brass punctured by minute lenses, is an eye with a memory, an archetypal door that hints at things beyond what we can see, things that stir the imagination. As in several of his recent projects, Pallasmaa isolates the door to intensify its presence, unlocking this simple plane's potential as a boundary, a passage, and an arrival: he elevates the door from a thing of use to a poetic object. On the other side of this door, unlike so many modern doors, it is clear that one has arrived in a place.

Signs of the Finnish origin of the institute can be seen in the wood used throughout the interior in ceilings, doors, floors, furniture, and stair steps. Sensuous surfaces, elaboration of detail, a variety of textures and colors, and a feeling for the material suggest the traditions of a wood culture. At the same time that the modular structure of the exterior hints at a universal approach it also recalls centuries of asceticism in Finnish design.

Reacting to the multifaceted program, the architects approached a number of chal-

Elevation

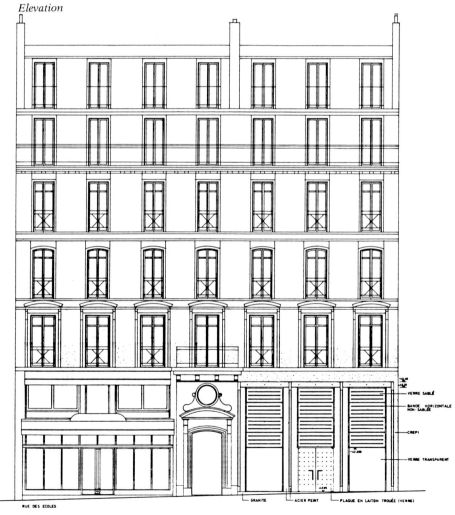

lenges—limitations of space and the density of technical systems—through a scale between that of a building and that of furniture. In this respect, the architects' meticulous attention to detail was comparable to the design of ship interiors. The tactile qualities and the small scale of the interior give it a sense of coziness that is hardly implied by the austere image of the institute's façade.

Transparency and continuity between rooms have been emphasized, visually enlarging the small scale of the interior. A highly detailed staircase of beech wood and black steel, for example, unites all three floors at the points of entrance.

In terms of Pallasmaa's theoretical development, the Finnish Institute is an extension of his rational approach and its intersection with the sensual dimension. In one small building, archetypes, memory, a considered relation to the city, and a neofunctional approach to the program combine to make a dense architectural form.

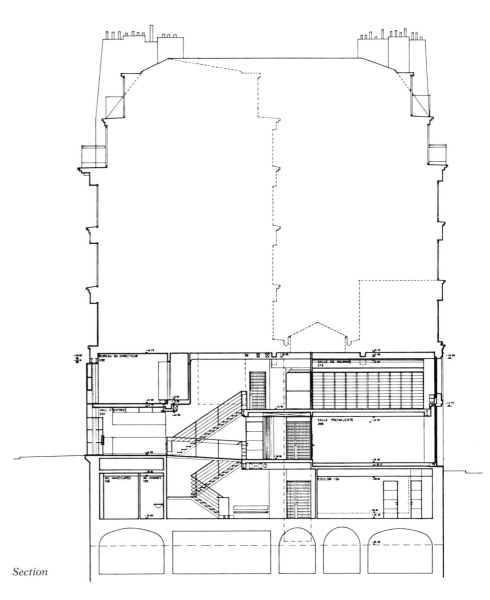

Section

Objects, Furniture, and Graphics

For over ten years, beginning in the early 1970s, Juhani Pallasmaa removed himself from the practice of architecture. During that time he published numerous articles on the theory and philosophy of architecture, served on competition juries, organized international symposia, and taught briefly in Europe, Africa, and America. While he was director of the Museum of Finnish Architecture from 1978 to 1983, he refined his artistic talents primarily through graphics and design. His exhibition designs in particular have kept him in close contact with architecture. While Pallasmaa continued to design exhibits, edit and lay out books, write articles, and lecture in the 1980s, his focus shifted to architecture, object, and furniture design.

Between 1983 and 1986 Pallasmaa completed the renovation of three buildings: the garret of a block of flats designed by Gesellius, Lindgren, and Saarinen, the Marimekko shop on the esplanade in Helsinki, and the transformation of a bus depot into an art museum in Rovaniemi. In each of these projects one has the sense that every screw and nail has been considered. However, in contrast to his early exploration in modular and prefabricated construction, the only standard, modern-building supplies used in the renovation of the garret were screws and nails.

The relationship between matter and the hand was perhaps the most significant shift in Pallasmaa's thinking during his period of contemplation in the 1970s. Of the artist Raimo Utriainnen, Pallasmaa has written, "The sculptor's sense of form is just as much in his fingers and muscles as his eyes. He wrote further, "It is evident that in any form of art an incessant creative interaction between the artist and his work is essential."

Close contact with bronze, steel, glass, granite, and wood added a sensual dimension to Pallasmaa's rationalist approach. It also gave the architect a further degree of control in his projects. In the Marimekko shop, for example, the commission was expanded to include all the fittings of the shop: furnishings, light fixtures, door pulls, handles and knobs, tailor's dummies, the clothes-hanging system, packaging supplies, carrier bags, and shop signs.

Pallasmaa's interest in furniture parallels his approach to architecture. Often a relation is established between contrasting materials, such as the metal and wood of his steel-and-ash chair, in which qualities of hardness and strength are set in opposition to

tactility, warmth, and softness. At other times, Pallasmaa's objects can suggest poetic images, such as light opening the leaves of a book or aerial images of fluttering wings. Typically his furniture and objects are sparse, but upon close examination they reveal the effort involved in works that achieve simplicity.

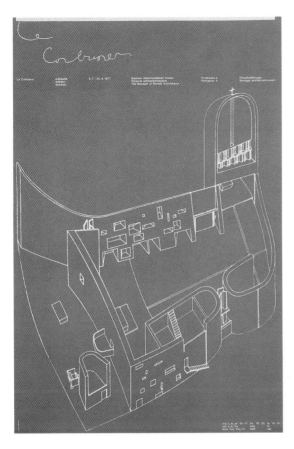

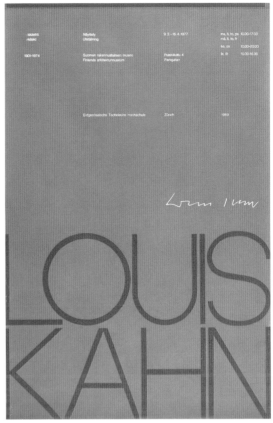

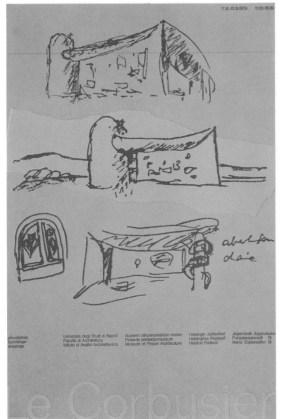

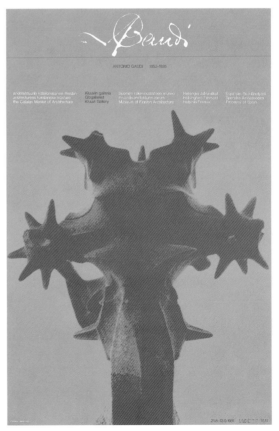

JUHA LEIVISKÄ

German Embassy • Kuusisaari, Helsinki • 1992

The site for the new German Embassy is on the south beach of a wooded island, facing Helsinki's archipelago. Leiviskä divided the site into four parts, marked by the wings of the embassy building. Through this gesture, he preserved the existing gardens from a villa demolished in 1970 and distinguished the private and public realms of the embassy. Between the two wings, whose backs almost touch, the walls frame views of gardens and the wooded landscape, as well as vistas of the sea and nearby islands.

The interior spatial arrangement has been guided by a similar principle, opening the rooms to

views of each other and vistas of the sea. Framing the landscape, the freestanding walls, which contain service elements, such as ventilation ducts, also provide a background for works of art. To date, the embassy is one of Leiviskä's most ambitious architectural compositions.

Second floor plan

Ground floor plan

Church and Parish Center • Myyrmäki, Vantaa • 1984

For Juha Leiviskä, an architect whose buildings combine aspects of Aulis Blomstedt's rationalist thinking with the sensuality of Aalto's architecture, the straight lines of the plane are an obsession. Since the 1960s Leiviskä has relentlessly pursued an architecture of walls and the possibility of dematerializing construction with light. Few motifs, the tension of the horizontal and the vertical, and a series of relations based on a module and its multiples characterize his work. He confessed to a colleague that, in regard to external form, "I have the feeling that I keep on drawing the same building."

At the same time, Leiviskä has said, "I believe in the permanency of the basic factors in architecture. . . . I do not therefore believe that there has been anything in recent years which could revolutionize the basic tenets of architecture or its central task."

The Myyrmäki Church and Parish Center were designed as a vessel for holding light. Inside the parish hall, the feeling of distance and a consciousness of infinity dominate the room. The altar, placed along the long wall in the shallow dimension of the sanctuary, is framed by a constant, glowing light. Like the *transparente* in a baroque church, there is an illusion of depth created by an unseen source of illumination. The dynamic spatial effects within this room of planes allow Leiviskä to achieve his aim of producing a "shimmering, constantly changing veil of light."

Leiviskä exaggerates the wall's planar quality by allowing light to fall on the planes themselves. Flat, white surfaces and light dissolve the weight and materiality of the wall, but shadows understate its singularity.

Walls protect the Myyrmäki Church and Parish Center. They cut the interior off from what Leiviskä refers to as the visual pollution of the nearby high-rise housing and from the railway that runs along the length of the building, less than fifteen meters from the altar. While some of Leiviskä's walls close and cut off, others open and embrace, as do the shorter walls perpendicular to the park.

With baroque exuberance and calm Nordic control, Juha Leiviskä creates in the Myyrmäki Church a delicate setting for one of Finland's most precious commodities: light.

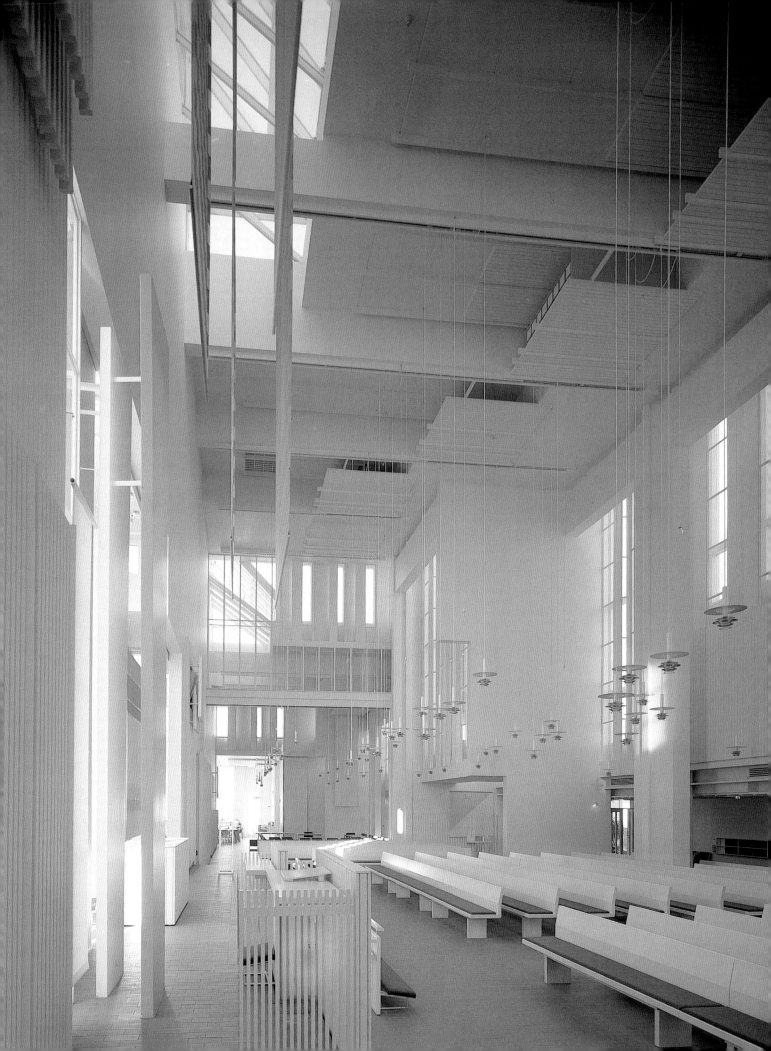

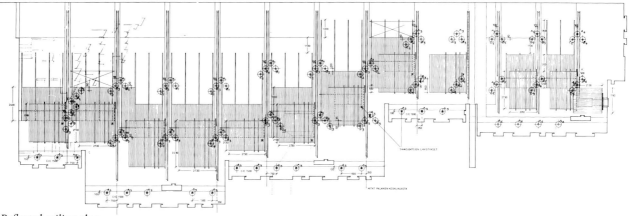

Reflected ceiling plan

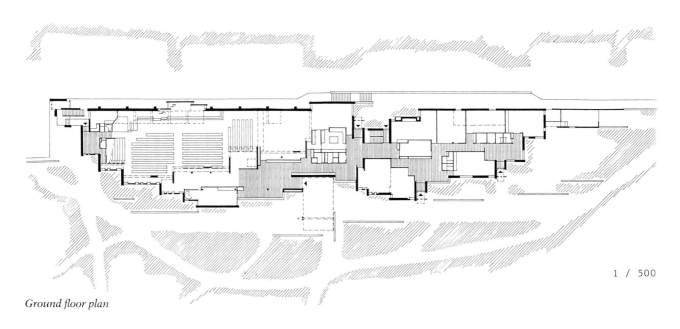

1 / 500

Ground floor plan

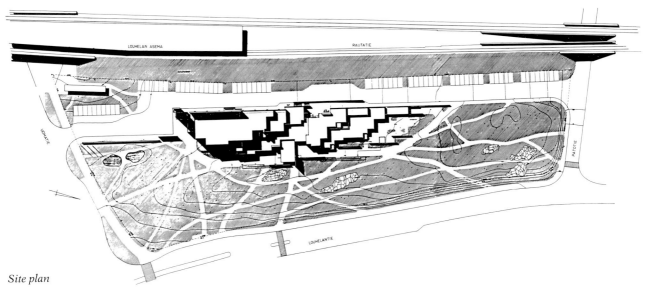

Site plan

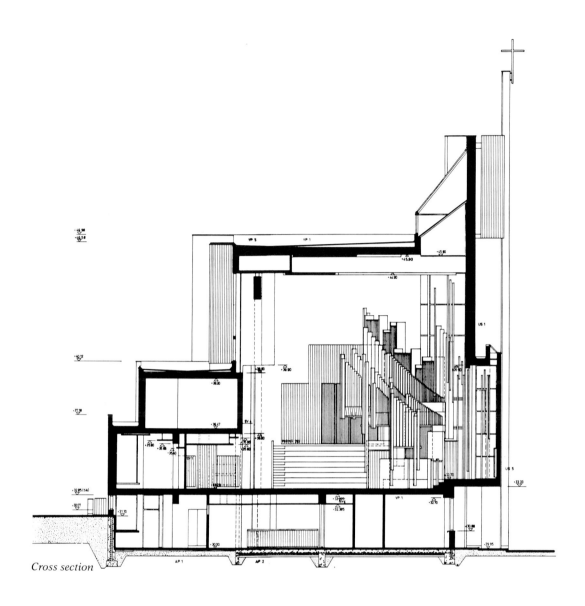

Cross section

Art Museum • Kajaani • designed 1985–1988

At the edge of a sloping site facing the Kajaaninjoki River, Leiviskä has designed a museum as a chain of rooms that control the landscape and collect light. Designed as part of a cultural complex planned by Sinikka Kouvu and Erkki Partanen, the museum was positioned lower than the existing buildings so that it would act as a plinth, emphasizing their importance.

Entry to the building is from an upper piazza, with the main galleries on a lower floor along the edge of the hillside. The sweeping vista of the river is closed by the mass of the building from the piazza, but opened again with selected views between each of the five large gallery rooms. As in many of Leiviskä's buildings, a large, overall scale has been adapted to the terrain through a series of repetitive gestures. The section is designed in such a way that the clerestories only admit reflected light. Its complexity rivals some of Alvar Aalto's most extraordinary sections.

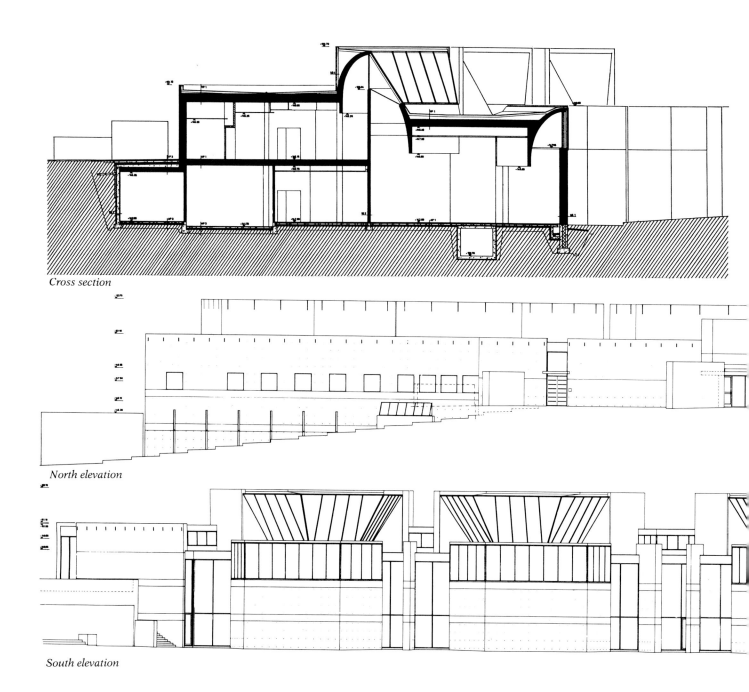

Cross section

North elevation

South elevation

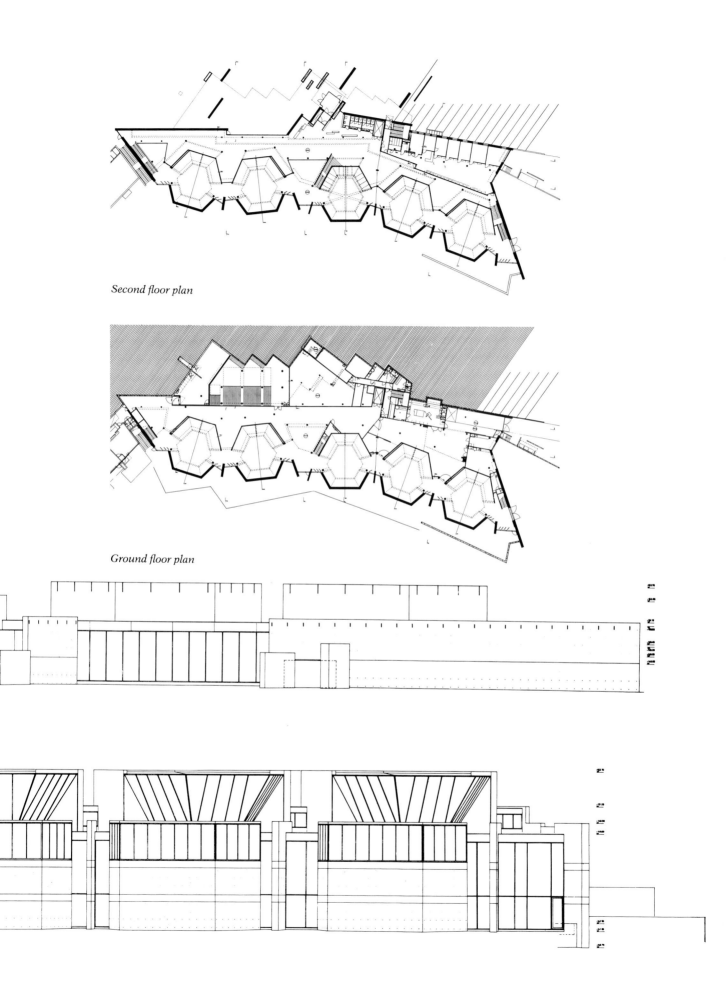

Second floor plan

Ground floor plan

Parish Center • Kirkkonummi • 1984

Built along the southern slope of the vicarage hill in Kirkkonummi, the parish center is oriented toward the town center and a thirteenth-century church. The Pappilanmäki Vicarage, a low complex of residential buildings, and a new housing development were freely arranged along the lower slope, leaving the long hill free. Leiviskä felt that the hill would constitute the heart of the architecture, and he designed a linear building that was positioned to frame the hill and stress the dynamics of the slope.

History is a central influence in Leiviskä's work. His debt to the planar architectural forms of de Stijl is clear, but the imagery of more remote artistic sources in his

work is less apparent. For example, Leiviskä describes the stepping room arrangement of the Kirkkonummi Parish Center as "reminiscent of ancient monasteries in southern and eastern Europe, where a compact block of long, horizontal sections and walls is rhythmically divided."

Leiviskä is well aware of the limited themes in his work, but feels that this does not exclude counterpoint. His description of the contrapuntal, polyphonic composition of the fugue is perhaps close to the composition of his own work: "Each voice enters at its own point and frequently at its own pitch . . . the impression is one of the voices chasing each other, a network is created."

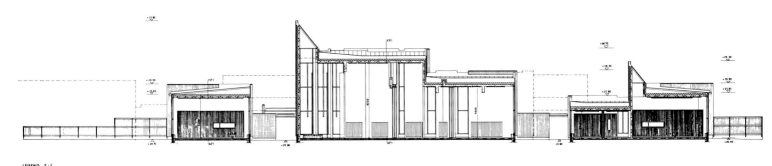

LEIKKAUS F - F

Section

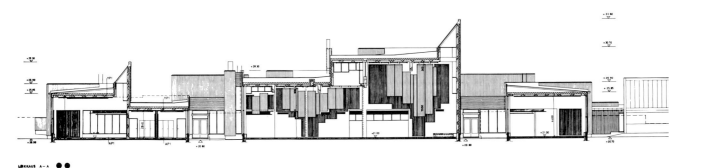

LEIKKAUS A - A ● ●

Section

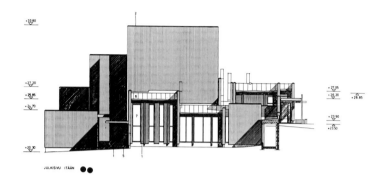

Elevation

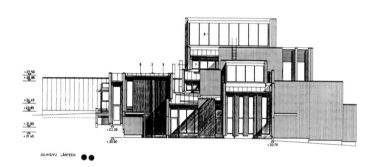

Elevation

Männistö Church • 1992

The Männistö Church is based on principles of spatial arrangement and light that were developed in the Myyrmäki and Kirkkonummi projects, which had their beginnings as early as 1968 in Leiviskä's competition design for a cemetery and chapels in Vaasa.

Here, as in those earlier projects, the modulation of walls, their relationship with the site, and their determination of interior space give form to the architecture. The living interaction of light and a room is central to Leiviskä's work. Like Nils Erik Wickberg's description of the late baroque churches of south Germany, Leiviskä's architecture is an instrument for light to play on.

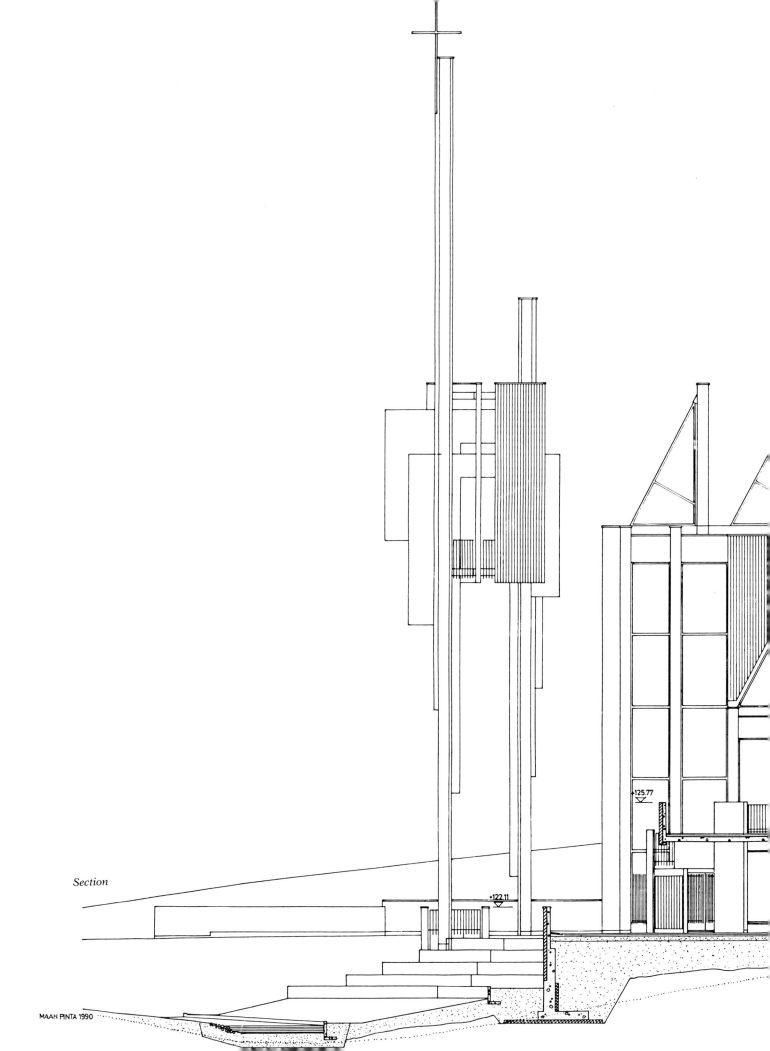

Section

+125.77

+122.11

MAAN PINTA 1990

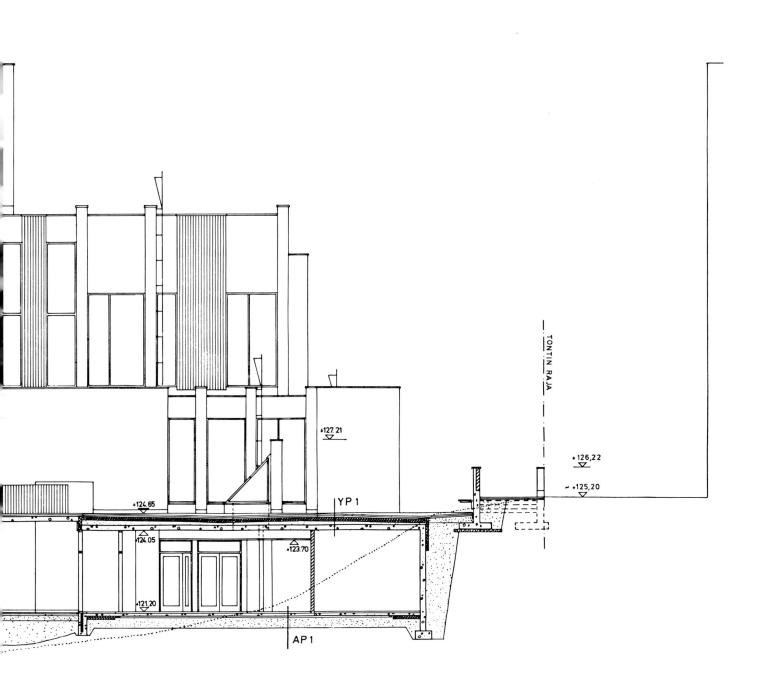

TONTIN RAJA

+127.21

+126,22

~ +125,20

YP 1

+124.65

+124.05

+123.70

+121.20

AP 1

ARTO SIPINEN

Cultural Center • Espoo, Tapiola • 1989

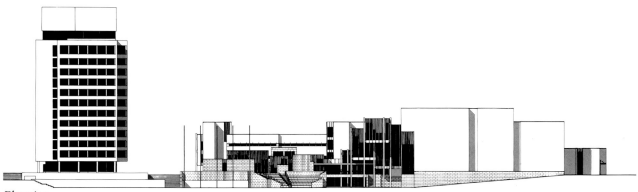

Elevation

Begun in 1952, the new town of Tapiola, located eight kilometers west of Helsinki, became internationally recognized as a model for satellite town planning. Aarne Ervi won the competition for the town center in 1954, and today the Espoo Cultural Center occupies a critical position in that plan. A flat plane of water and a tower were the primary forms that ordered the 1954 plan; in 1961 both designs were completed by Ervi. In the mid-1960s a hotel with a swimming pool also designed by Aarne Ervi created a degree of spatial definition on the west end of the water basin, but for nearly twenty-five years the northwest

edge of the site was unoccupied.

Arto Sipinen's competition entry recognized the architectural importance of the site's structure by giving the large, multifunction cultural center a relatively small scale. Diminishing the scale of the cultural center with a field of vertical elements, the transparency of glass, and a horizontal base that holds stairs, an amphitheater, and a waterfall allowed Sipinen to emphasize the dominance of Ervi's tower and form an outdoor room adjacent to the water basin.

A dramatic shift in scale occurs at the line of points that separates the southern part of the

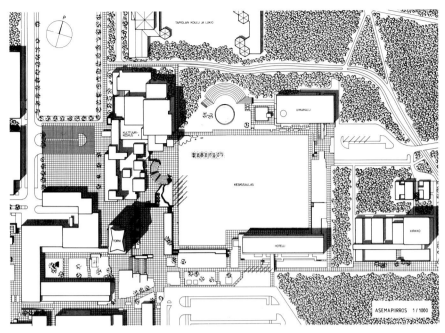

Site plan

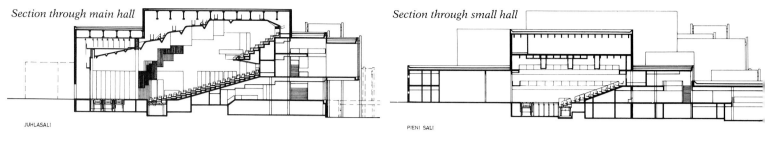

Section through main hall

JUHLASALI

Section through small hall

PIENI SALI

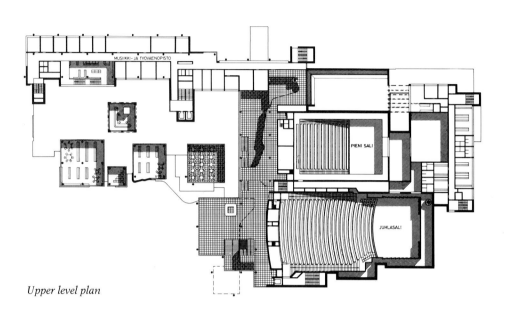

Upper level plan

Site plan and lower level plan

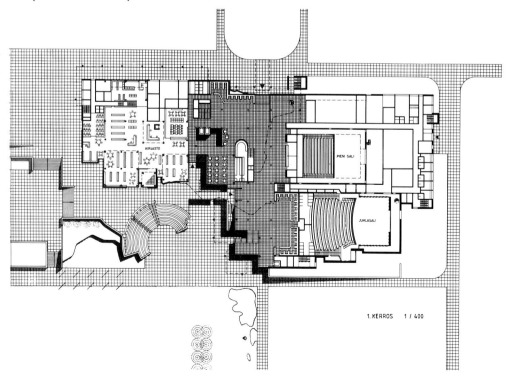

1. KERROS   1 / 400

building's column structure from the wall structure that forms the two large halls and the exhibition room. The column structure gave Sipinen the flexibility to accommodate the large number of diverse functions—lobby, foyer, library, music classrooms, worker's institute, and café. He was thus able to articulate this complexity in the massing of the building, at the same time maintaining the architectonic integrity of the whole as the building is animated by the light.

Whiteness also unifies the form. Inside and out, layers of white quartz, sandstone, and Roman travertine tiles cover concrete floors and walls in the manner of white paint. In this way the architecture of the cultural center resembles the assemblage technique of Louise Nevelson, particularly on a white Nordic day when the glass reflects a cloudy sky.

Hierarchically, Sipinen chose to give dominance to the lobby, which is perhaps one of the

most important public rooms in Tapiola. While the building sustains a number of major cultural events, such as the opera, theater, and concerts, the daily use of the lobby as an interior public room—

especially in the cold of a Finnish winter—gives added civic importance to a building that is already a base for the performing arts in Espoo.

The concert hall, which seats 812 people (613 in the stalls and 199 in the balcony), was designed especially for the demands of orchestra, opera, and choir performances. It features excellent acoustics and a completely silent ventilation system that operates by means of ducts in the seating. Visually, the room has a quality of absolute calmness, as if it were waiting for an event to occur. Adjacent to the concert hall a theater (189–442 seats) was designed primarily for dramatic purposes, but it can also be adapted for experimental theater, concerts, films, and conferences.

As a series of functional events, the cultural center fulfills its purpose well, but as an addition to the urban fabric of Tapiola its public rooms are an outstanding accomplishment.

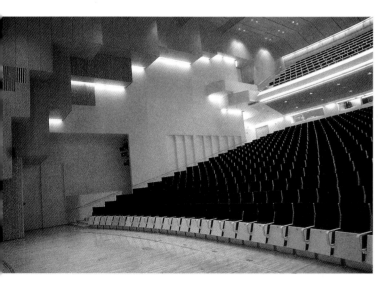

Concert Hall • Mikkeli • 1988

Unlike the Espoo Cultural Center, which adjusts and defines an existing urban condition, the Mikkeli Concert Hall was built one kilometer from the town center and is completely surrounded by nature. The main features of the concert hall are the transparency of the foyer, its internal vistas, and its interchange with the small lake, Pankalampi. From the ground to the roof, glass walls open to the south and reflect the earth and sky just as the water reflects the building.

The Mikkeli Concert Hall is less complex in terms of program than Sipinen's Espoo building, but it is based upon similar architectural principles. Like the earlier design, columns separate and distinguish the open public areas from the walls that enclose the functional component of the concert hall. The functional aspect of the building is not only revealed in structure but also in terms of massing. From the exterior, a functional hierarchy is clearly established between the large halls that are the core of the building and the surrounding elements that support the primary mass. In this sense Sipinen's work continues the tradition of white cubist functionalism introduced to Finland in the late 1920s most conspicuously through the work of Alvar Aalto.

Although Arto Sipinen's early work, such as his highly regarded Jyväskylä Library, exhibited a Miesian approach to structure and detailing, his recent work reflects the influence of Aalto as well as a neofunctional approach.

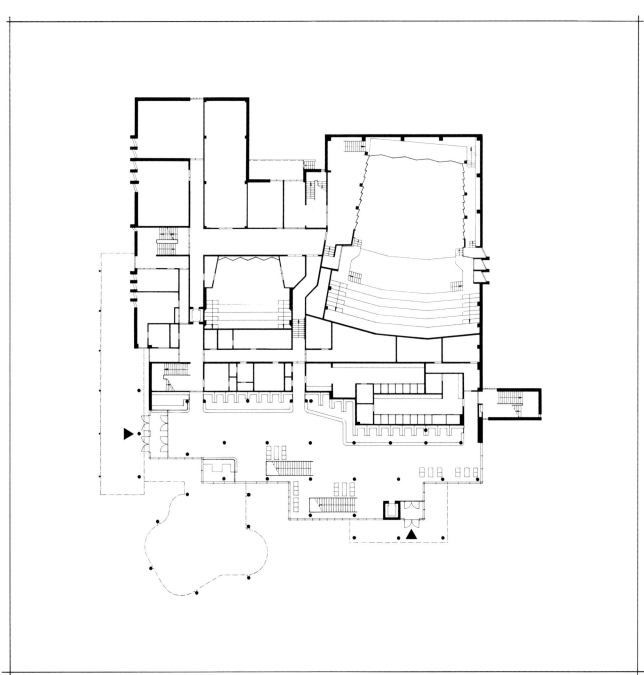

Lower level plan

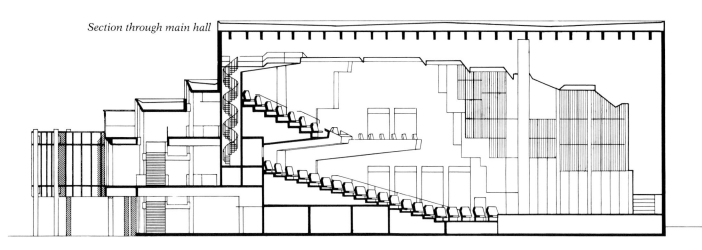

Section through main hall

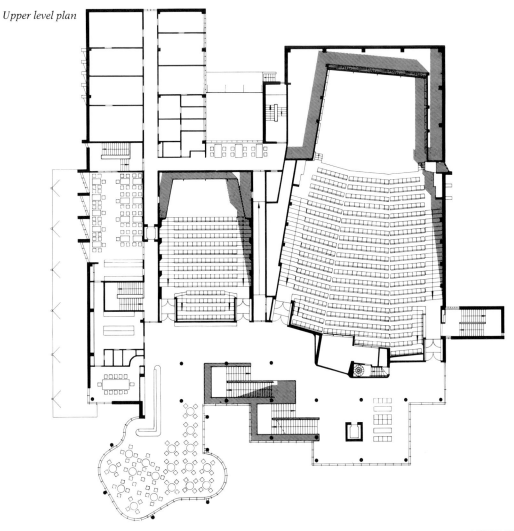

Upper level plan

New Helsinki Center • Kamppi-Töölönlahti • 1985

Beginning with C. L. Engell in the early 1800s, urban plans have been designed for the void between the Töölönlahti and Eläintarhanlahti bays in Helsinki. Eliel Saarinen, Bertel Jung, Oiva Kallio, J. S. Sirén, P. E. Blomstedt, Yrjö Lindegren, and Kaija and Heikki Sirén are among the noted architects who have proposed plans for the site in this century.

Alvar Aalto made three proposals for the site between 1959 and 1975, which were characterized by a chain of public buildings on the west bank of Töölönlahti Bay, a motorway paralleling the railway line, and a series of concrete terraces on Töölönlahti Bay's southern rim, opening vistas to the north. In the late 1960s construction was begun on Finlandia Hall, which was one of several cultural buildings Aalto planned for the west

bank of Töölönlahti Bay. Aalto focused some of the views from the main lobby of Finlandia Hall on the disarray of the railway service yard, which he once called Helsinki's "internal crater," understating the inappropriateness of this function on such a critical site and underscoring the importance of future development.

As a student in the late 1950s Arto Sipinen worked in Alvar Aalto's office and participated in the planning of the New Helsinki Center. Over twenty-five years later, in 1985, Sipinen entered his own plan for the New Helsinki Center in an open competition and was awarded a divided first prize, which was shared with the architect Jan Söderland and the architectural team of Kari Mökkääla and Ilmo Valjakka.

Sipinen's plan envisioned a

highly developed pedestrian system that linked the Kamppi and Töölönlahti areas at the Parliament Building and east-west connections between the Töölönlahti and Eläintarhanlahti bays by building over the railway tracks north of the station. The scale of the projected urban spaces, like those south of Finlandia Hall and east of the Parliament Building, was particularly strong in Sipinen's plan, as was the thought of bringing the water, which once flowed from the bay to the sea, back into the city.

From the indecisive moment of the competition judgment in 1986, plans for the area have been clouded by bureaucratic struggles, and there is presently no comprehensive plan for the future of a site that over 500,000 people pass through daily.

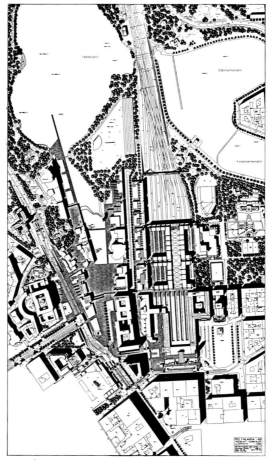

Site plan

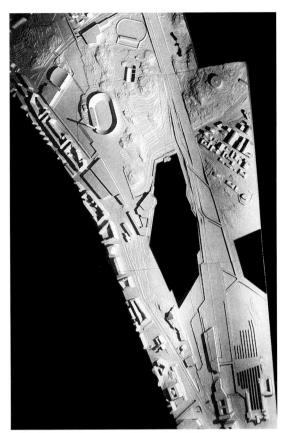

Alvar Aalto, "New Center Helsinki," 1973

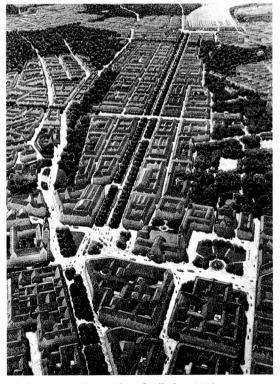

Eliel Saarinen, "Pro Helsingfors" plan, 1918

PEKKA HELIN AND TUOMO SIITONEN

Center for Changing Exhibitions • Helsinki • mid-1990s

The Center for Changing Exhibitions was originally designed to meet the requirements of a spacious, international exhibition facility. Recently, however, plans for a new museum of contemporary art in Helsinki have allowed the exhibition facility to become an extension shared jointly by the Museum of Finnish Architecture and the Museum of Applied Arts.

By making the new extension half a story underground, Tuomo Siitonen accommodated the large mass of the exhibition hall, allowed the two existing nineteenth-century buildings already protected by the National Board of Antiquities to maintain their identity, and provided an opportunity for a strong image in the center of the block. By drawing back the smaller mass of the new facility from both the existing buildings and the street, Siitonen further defined the new building as an object.

Two large concrete walls with glass on their outer edges contain the entrance hall to the new exhibition facility. Together with a pair of triangular skylights that frame the entrance from Ullulinnankatu, the glass entry hall forms a luminous entity which takes advantage of the darkness that dominates the late fall, winter, and early spring in Helsinki.

Siitonen's approach recalls the tradition of clarity and restraint that characterized much of the best Finnish architecture of the 1950s and 1960s. When Aarno Ruusuvuori was designing the Tapiola church in the early 1960s, he described this building as "no more than a dark shadow among the pines." Tuomo Siitonen's Center for Changing Exhibitions, like his former professor's church, is a humble addition to the museum block—little more than two walls and some light in the dark.

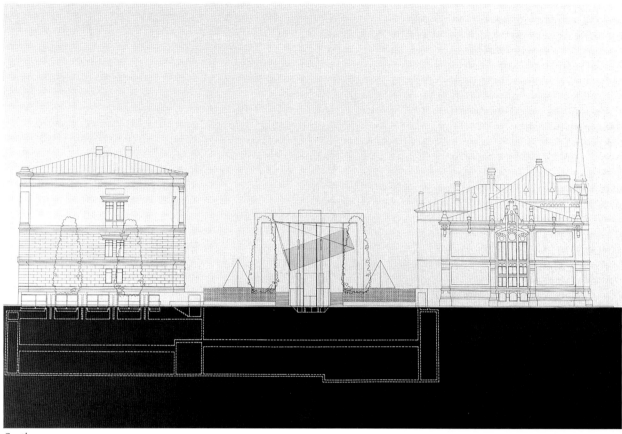

Section

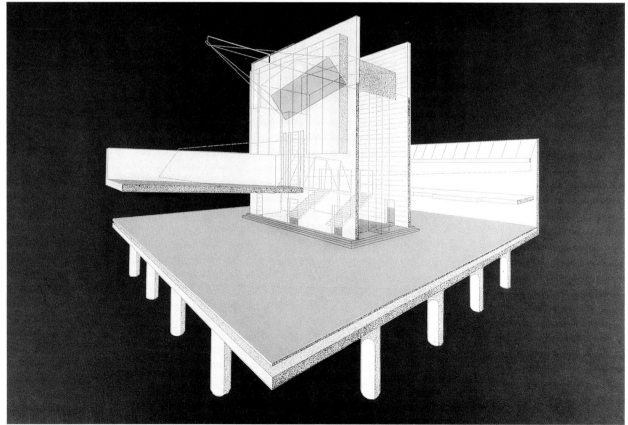

Cutaway axonometric

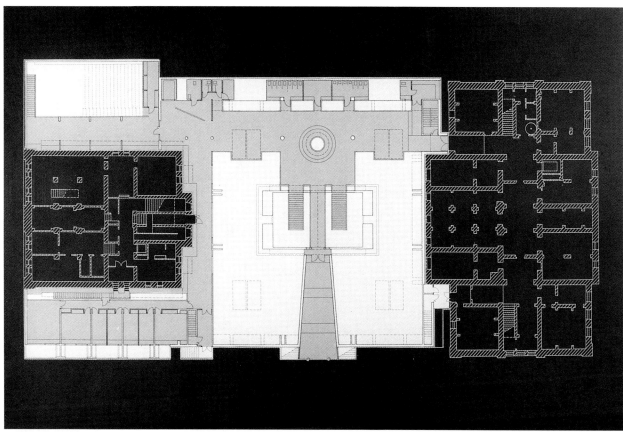

Upper level plan

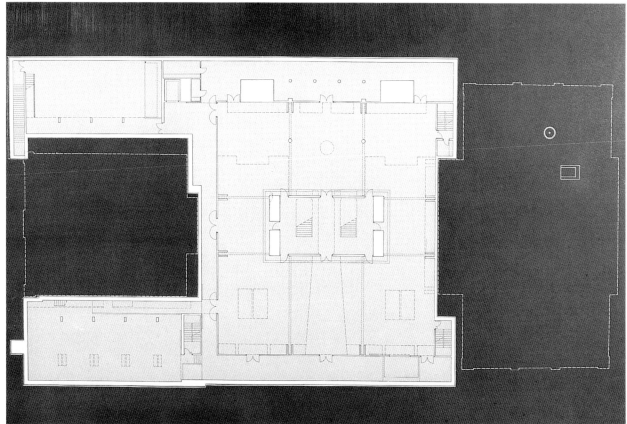

Lower level plan

Ekono OTA/IV Office Building • Espoo • 1990

Tuomo Siitonen's recent office building for the Ekono Company was designed to anticipate future trends in office construction. The most distinctive feature of the design is the EKOFLOOR, a structure suspended from columns. Half the thickness of a conventional in situ cast slab, the EKOFLOOR system consists of a slab that serves as a ceiling for the lower area and a series of supports that bear on the suspended slab, allowing for an access floor that houses mechanical and structural systems between the slab and the space of the office.

The combination of a suspended bearing floor and an access floor offers a degree of flexibility not found in conventional office construction. All of the utilities can be easily reached under the floor through a system of removable plates that consti-tute the office-floor surface. The easy accessibility to utilities allows the offices to be continually updated as new technologies are applied to the system. Cabling is installed under the access floor with connections that allow for the modification of new or existing equipment. Optical cabling, at the core of the information network, can be used for both large-scale applications and the development of information technology in the building. The largely prefabricated building also features automatic house management, security systems, and an air-conditioning system that can be controlled in individual rooms. The form of the building and its spatial configuration are designed to accommodate future needs and allow for the application of innovative technology.

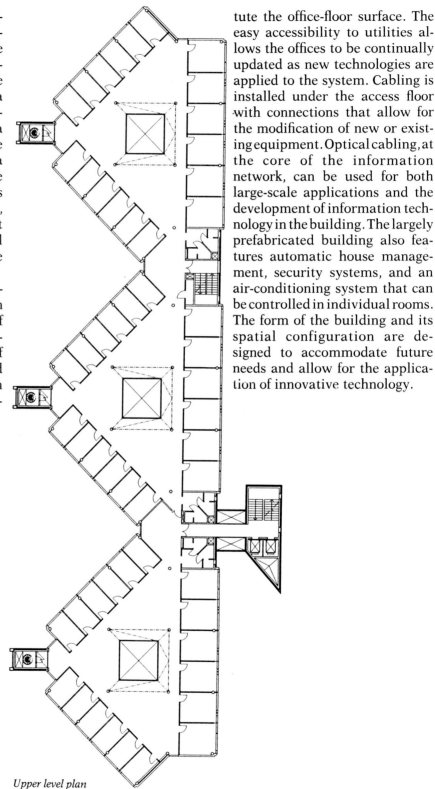

Upper level plan

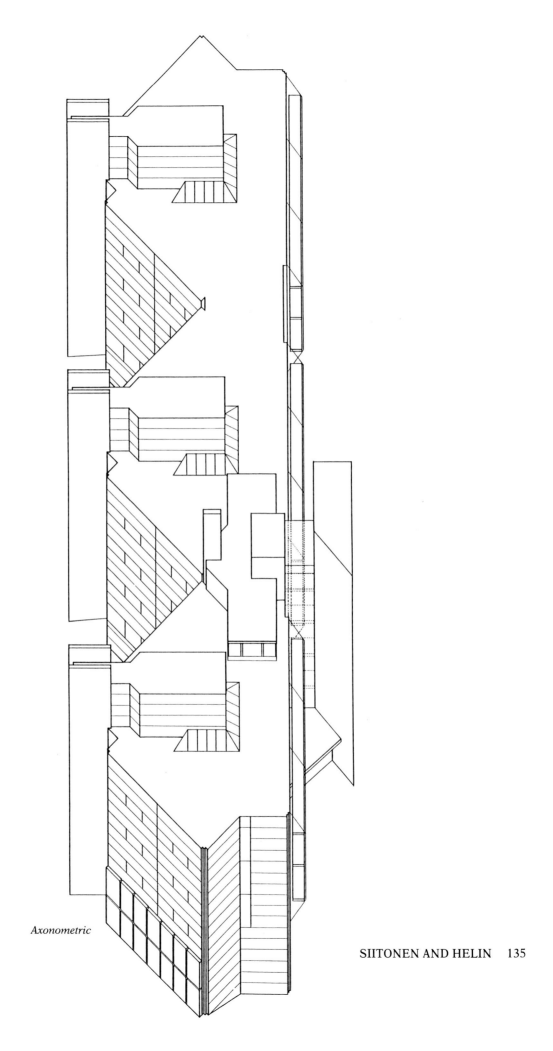

Axonometric

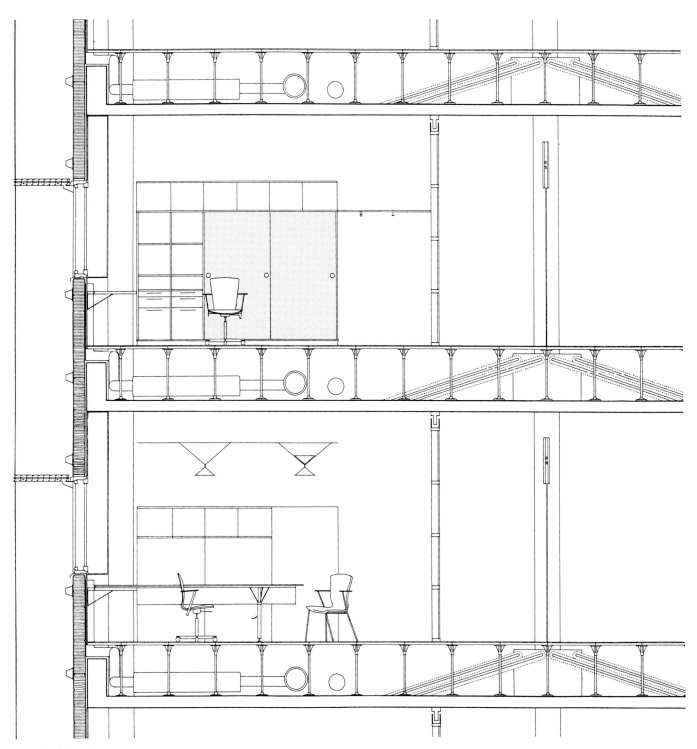

Partial section

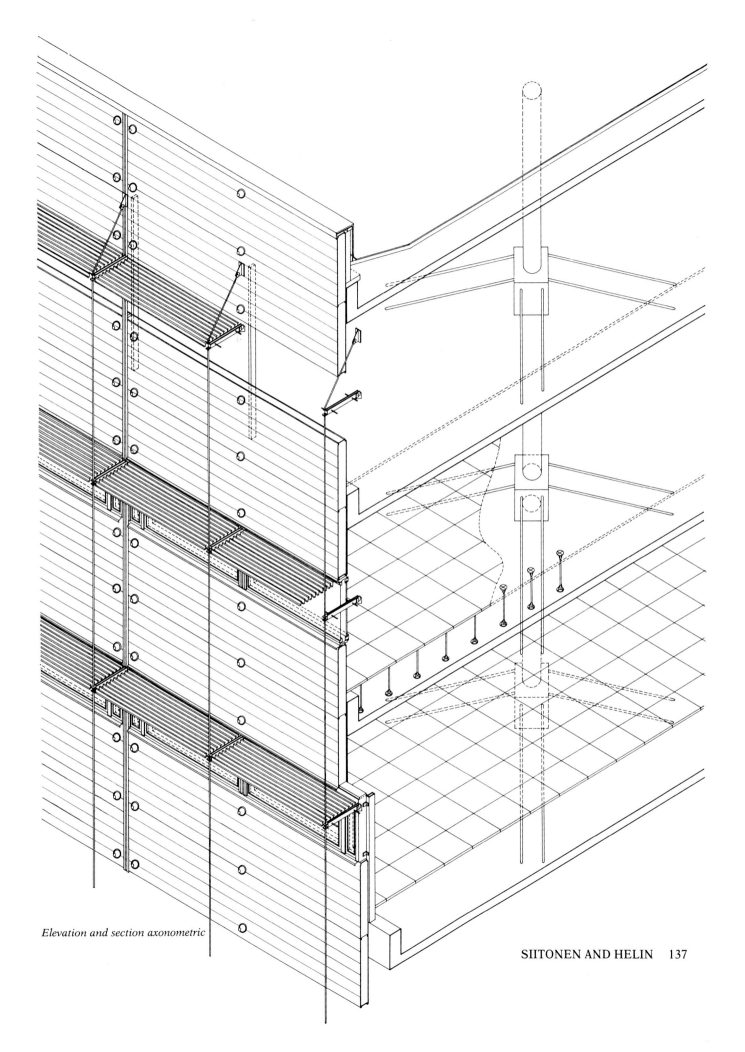

Elevation and section axonometric

Carbon-Fiber Chair • 1988

Although it has not been commercially produced, Tuomo Siitonen's carbon-fiber chair was developed coincident with the first carbon-fiber chairs now marketed in Europe. With the assistance of the Finnish manufacturer Excel and a government grant, Siitonen produced the first prototype in 1988, when he was invited to participate in a competition for innovative furniture design. Excel, a sports-equipment firm owned by the Nesté Company, already had experience working with carbon fiber in its line of world-renowned ski poles, and offered the assistance of its engineers to develop the chair design.

The result was a strong, light (1.8 kilogram) chair with low conductivity, a dynamic form, and an assembly technique suitable for mass production. But it was expensive. The mold for the prototype cost 17,000 FMK (approximately $4,700), and the carbon-fiber material to produce a single chair was 800 FMK (approximately $220). Like Siitonen's most recent architecture, the chair is a minimalist form based on a clear conception.

Experimental Housing • Borås, Hestra, Sweden • 1990

Borås, Hestra, was the site of an experimental housing project based on principles similar to those of Tapiola Garden City, outside Helsinki. Pekka Helin's project (Borås A) was begun with the notion that the 1990s call for a new approach to planning and new housing solutions. High-rise housing, he feels, has particularly fallen behind the design standards of low-rise housing. Helin believes new features of improved highrise housing would be a more functional approach, more oppor-

tunities for light, larger balconies and terraces, and a more striking appearance.

The dynamic form of Helin's introverted, wedge-shaped atrium house contrasts vividly with Tuomo Siitonen's approach (Borås B), which relies on the development of spatial aspects within a standard economical framework. Long internal vistas, split levels on the top and bottom stories, and a balcony terrace set apart from the main mass of the building create an effect of spa-

ciousness within a relatively small area in Siitonen's design. A utility core, located close to the balcony terrace, allows the area to be used flexibly, as an outdoor grill, a greenhouse, or a sauna with an open fireplace, for example. In both Helin and Siitonen's projects, the notion of a modern, highly functional, well-lit housing unit, adaptable to a variety of conditions, is at the center of their architecture.

Site plan (Borås A)

BORÅS HESTRA
BYGGFAST·H+S·FFNS/HUST
PERSPEKTIV
30.0

Cutaway interior perspective (Borås A)

Elevation (Borås A)

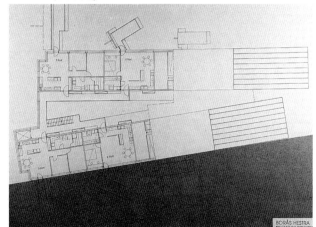

Lower level plan (Borås A)

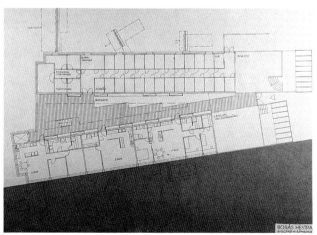

Upper level plan (Borås A)

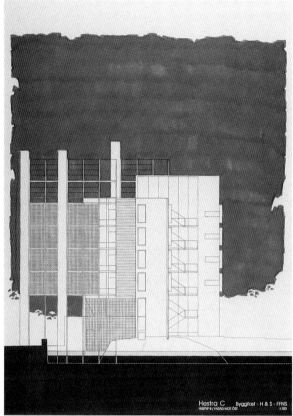

Elevation (Borås B)

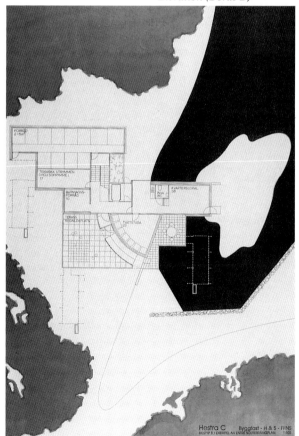

Floor plan (Borås B)

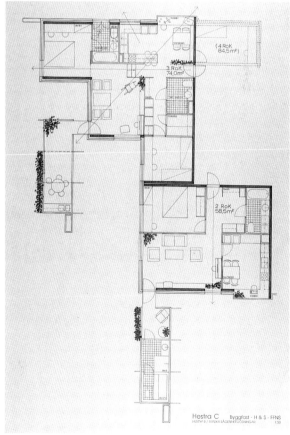

Floor plan (Borås B)

Swimming Hall and Multipurpose Center • Hollola • 1986

The fundamental idea for the swimming hall at Hollola was the image of a public bath interpreted through the language of modern architecture. Soft forms, light-colored wood, groupings of skylights, and columns rising out of the water contribute to a spa-like atmosphere rather than a high-performance training area.

The building includes youth facilities which are separated by an entrance foyer and café from the changing rooms of the swimming hall. In terms of construction, the bearing frame is formed by columns and walls cast in situ, while the external walls are constructed of prefabricated elements and covered with tiles.

Like many of Siitonen and Helin's plans from the mid-1980s onward, the architectural composition begins with elementary geometry, in this case a square supplemented by circles, which is elaborated from the details to the general massing of the building.

Pekka Helin has said that it is "most important to work for the integral, clear, authentic, minimal. People in the so-called developed world are beginning to be surrounded by an ever-increasing mass of junk, unnecessary goods and information." He goes on to say, "When there is too much noise one needs silence." Looking at the dressing room of Helin and Siitonen's swimming hall, one can clearly see a moment of constructed silence.

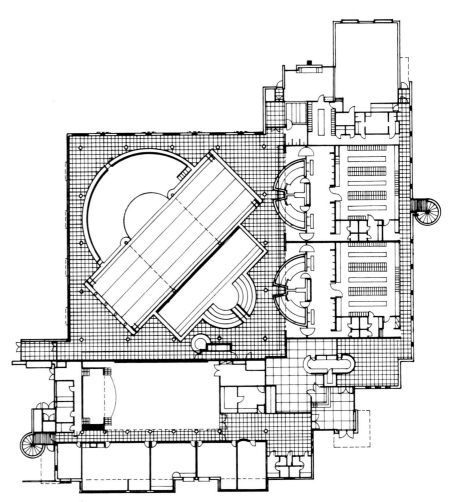

Ground floor plan

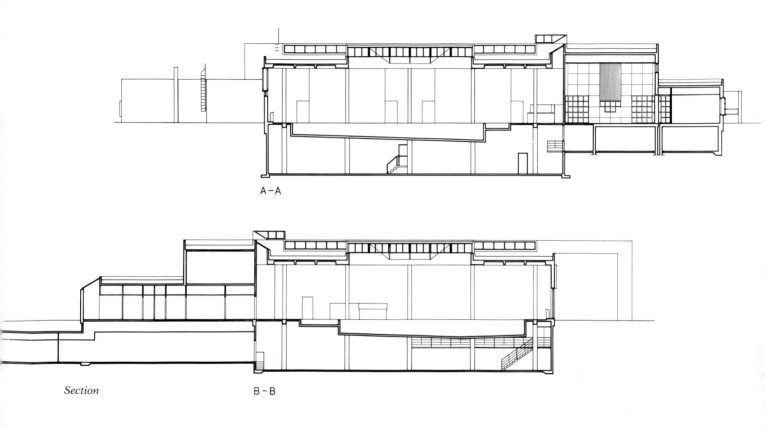

A–A

Section   B - B

EERO VALJAKKA

Lounaisrinne Housing • Jyväskylä • 1985

Following a period of almost unrestrained high-rise building in concrete in the 1960s and 1970s—a period of housing construction referred to in an essay by the architect Marja-Riitta Norri as "Prefabricated Madness"—the 1980s were a time when concrete and low-rise housing were reconsidered. In the early 1980s Eero Valjakka, along with the architects Jaako Laapotti, Pekka Helin, Timo Kauppinen, and Tuomo Siitonen, developed the Inhabitant BES (Concrete Unit System), a theoretical approach that defined new possibilities for concrete in housing. Eero Valjakka's practical application of those ideas were realized in an experimental housing estate in Jyväskylä in the mid-1980s.

Constructed of prefabricated hollow-core floor slabs, supported by concrete walls, built in situ, and clad in thermal concrete block, his low-rise housing recalls the optimistic functional period of the 1930s in Finland when concrete technology was widely employed in innovative projects. In contrast to that earlier time, however, combining prefabricated and hand-formed techniques allows for flexibility in the configuration of the housing and often reduces costs, an especially important consideration in state-

subsidized housing. Another significant development can be seen in the focus on the individual within the context of the housing complex. A variety of apartment types, terraces and balconies affording a maximum of sun and air, and considerations of privacy within a collective arrangement of units are features of Valjakka's project that separate his design from the type of standardized housing that had been severely criticized in Finland prior to the 1980s. His restrained use of color and material is a model for Finnish housing, particularly in a time of abundance.

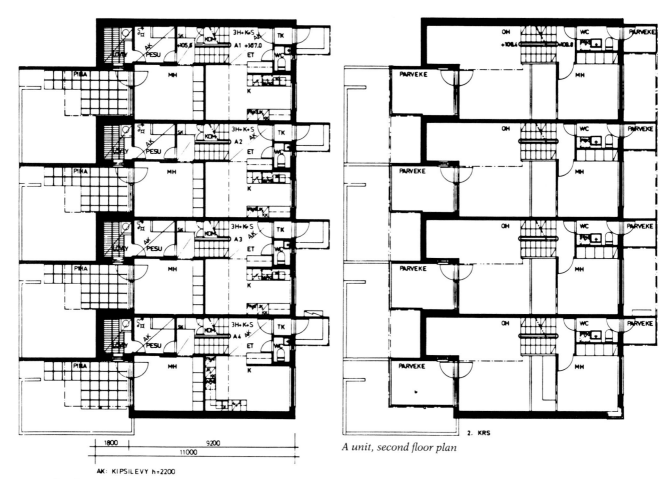

A unit, second floor plan

2. KRS

A unit, first floor plan

AK: KIPSILEVY h=2200

1800 9200
11000

Elevation

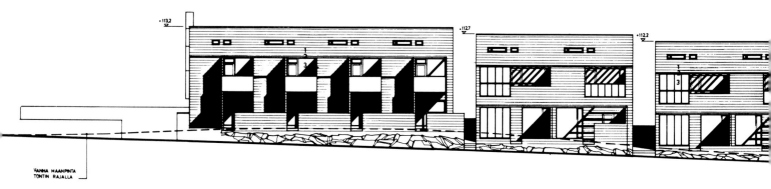

1 SLAMMATTU KEVYTSORAHARKKO,
   MAALATTU VALKOISEKSI
2 MAALATTU TERÄS
3 LASI

VANHA MAANPINTA
TONTIN RAJALLA

A   B   C

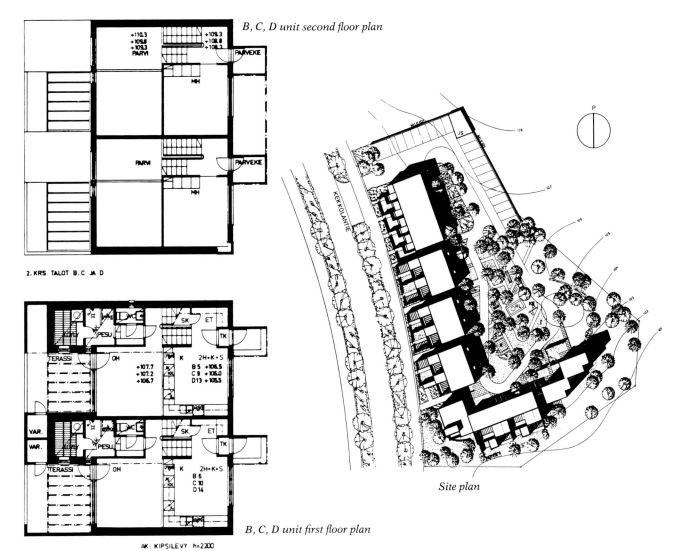

B, C, D unit second floor plan

2. KRS TALOT B.C JA D

Site plan

B, C, D unit first floor plan

AK: KIPSILEVY h=2200

1. KRS TALOT B.C JA D

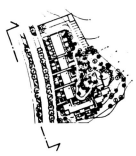

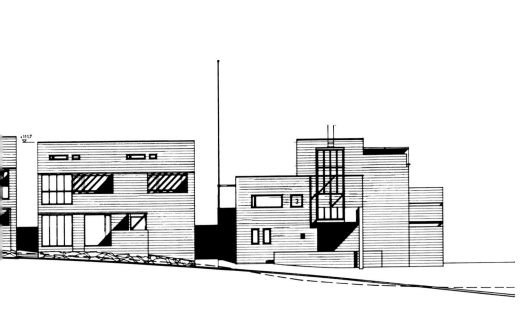

D   E   F

KEKKOLA 49	1		13
UUDISRAKENNUS		PAAPIRUSTUS	
AS.OY LOUNAISRINNE		TALOT A,B,C,D JA E-F 1:100 JULKISIVU LOUNAASEEN KEKKOLANT.	
ARKKITEHTUURITOIMISTO JÄRVINEN-VALJAKKA TÖÖLÖNKATU 11 00100 HELSINKI 10 PUH 446 698		154	13
HELSINKI 25.05.1984			

KARI JÄRVINEN AND TIMO AIRAS

Länsi-Säkylä Children's Day-Care Center • Säkylä,
Iso-Vimma • 1980

Themes of openness and closure, isolation and togetherness, and parts and whole are common to the housing, schools, nurseries, and day-care centers that have come from the office of Järvinen and Airas over the past ten years. Social engagement is one of their highest priorities. Both the children's day-care center and the Suna School combine the scale of the house, the sentimental invitation of the village, and interior spaces that resemble urban and rural models to enhance human communication in a familiar environment.

In the Säkylä Day-Care Center, light gives definition to an

LÄNSI-SÄKYLÄN PÄIVÄKOTI

1 DAY-CARE CENTRE
2 PARISH CLUB FACILITIES

Site plan

interior space around which the building is ordered. The ordering principle in the day-care center is a transformation of the rural courtyard, where functional entities are grouped around a core. Group facilities and the playroom are located within the interior courtyard while rest and activity rooms are situated facing an exterior courtyard to the south. The shape of the recurring, sloping roofs, the small scale, and the red-ocher color of the vertical weatherboarding also recall features from rural buildings, but they are reunited in a new form.

Säkylä Village is an old settlement along Pyhäjärvi Lake,

and the day-care center stands within a pine wood. Building the day-care center as a collection of familiar houses expressed the architect's intention to construct the locality. The memory of place is conspicuous in the architecture, and in retrospect the day-care center could be seen as a critical reaction to the placeless buildings that were pervasive not only in Finland, but in much of the Western world in the 1970s.

The overt regionalism of the 1980 day-care center is less apparent in Järvinen and Airas's more recent works where the duality of outer and inner is more important than the expression of local identity. In the Suna School a red-brick exterior acts as a crust for an inside whose texture is dissolved by white paint and light. The smooth, nearly uniform texture of the interior allows light and shade to clarify forms rather than material. Stairs, walls, and platforms in such an interior exaggerate the qualities of the most subtle light.

Balconies, overlooks, stairs, and arcades enrich the interior spaces of the Suna School and create an inside world that encourages a sense of community.

The model is a street. Along the street different places illuminated by skylight and defined by shadow allow for the individual and the collective in an environment that is more like a house than an institution. A stair, for example, allows for privacy and at the same time is an element of social engagement. In public buildings Järvinen and Airas's architecture reflects the paternal aspects of Finland's social democracy. In this sense it represents the society that commissioned the building.

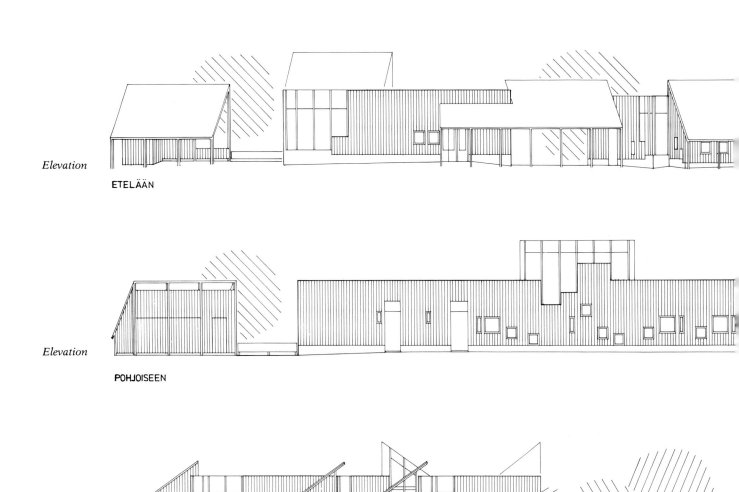

Elevation

ETELÄÄN

Elevation

POHJOISEEN

Elevation

ITÄÄN

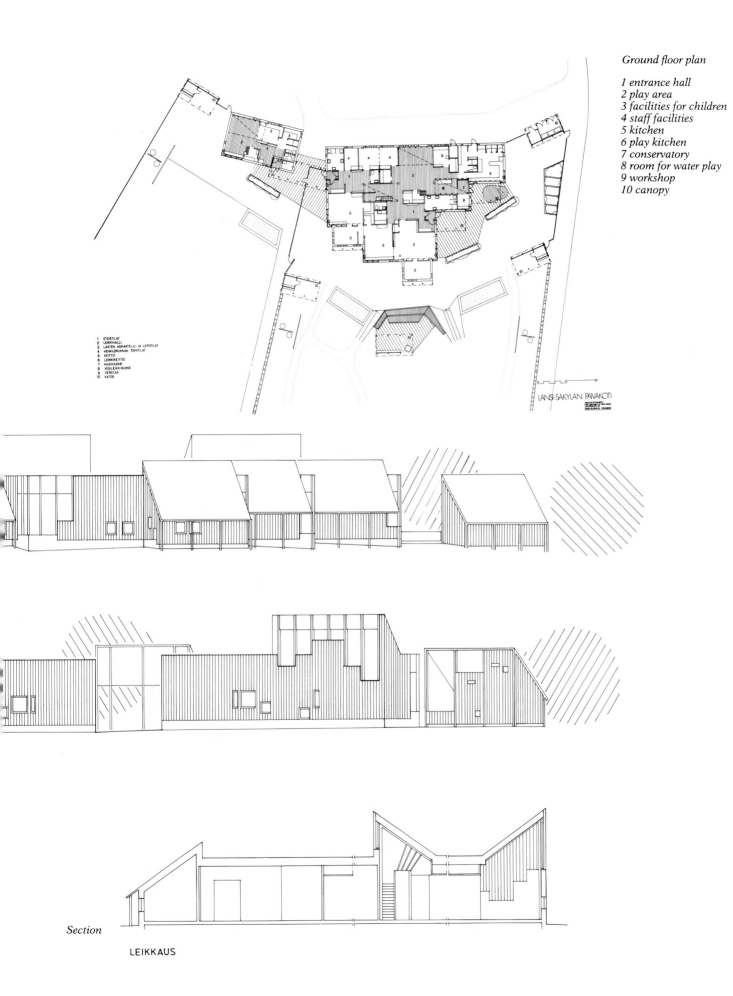

Ground floor plan

1 entrance hall
2 play area
3 facilities for children
4 staff facilities
5 kitchen
6 play kitchen
7 conservatory
8 room for water play
9 workshop
10 canopy

1   ETEISTILAT
2   LEIKKIHALLI
3   LASTEN ASKARTELU- JA LEPOTILAT
4   HENKILÖKUNNAN TOIMITILAT
5   KEITTIÖ
6   LEIKKIKEITTIÖ
7   KASVIHUONE
8   VESILEIKKIHUONE
9   VERSTAS
10 KATOS

LÄNSI-SÄKYLÄN PÄIVÄKOTI

Section

LEIKKAUS

Suna School • Espoo • 1985

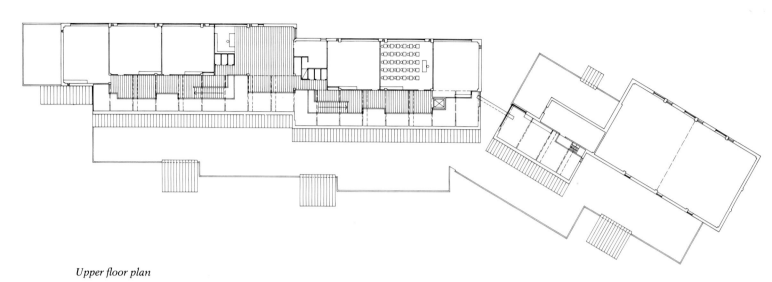

Upper floor plan

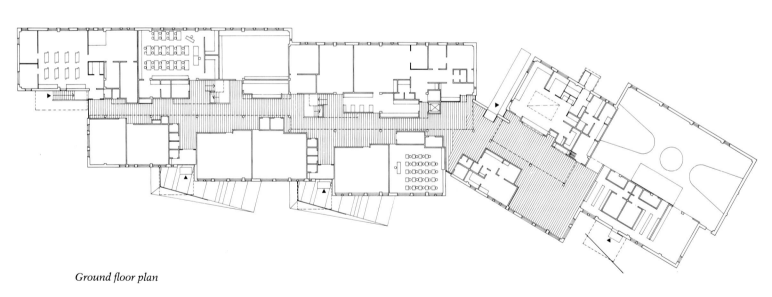

Ground floor plan

160   JÄRVINEN AND AIRAS

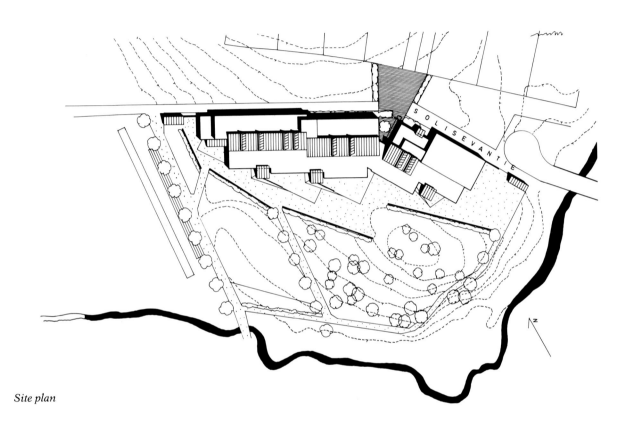

Site plan

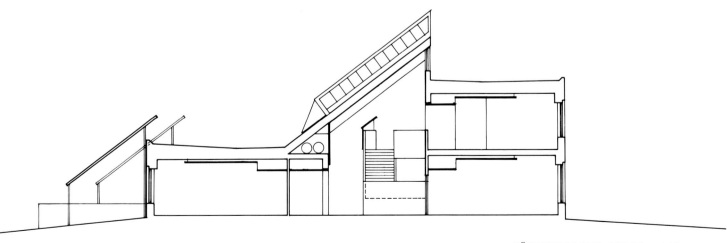

Section

MIKKO HEIKKINEN AND MARKKU KOMONEN

Heureka: The Finnish Science Center • Helsinki • 1988

When Mikko Heikkinen and Markku Komonen were awarded the commission for Heureka, the Finnish Science Center, they had already been working together for ten years at nights and on weekends while employed by other architects. This commission allowed them to form their own office; today they are at the forefront of Finnish architecture and the center of widespread international attention.

Heureka is located adjacent to Finland's busiest railway line, ten miles north of Helsinki in the suburb of Vantaa. Like many suburban building sites in Finland, Heureka's site was adjacent to an urban structure that fragmented as it approached the unbuilt landscape, in this case forest and farmland. To control the site the architects chose to reveal two aspects of the landscape that conspicuously illustrate the phenomena of nature and the control of that phenomena by man—the Kerava River and the railway line.

From the train, which carries twenty-five million people past the building in a single year, passengers glimpse the most sensual aspect of the building, a hundred-meter-long glass wall divided by the repetition of thirty-one steel struts according to the colors of the spectrum. This wall, like Louis Kahn's porches at the Kimbell Art Museum in Fort Worth, Texas, was an unprogrammed offering. "You know it wasn't programmed," Kahn said, "it is something that emerged."

The spectrum wall simulates one of nature's most stunning phenomena—the systematic division of visible light into colors. At the same time, it serves as a visual threshold that hints at the purpose of the building, which is to provide access to and rational interpretation of natural phenomena.

On the top floor the glass-and-steel wall screens an outdoor terrace, and in the original design there was an entry from the parking area crossing the railway and piercing the spectrum wall. Unfortunately, due to budget constraints, this entry was deleted from the project, although a fragment of this idea still remains in the observation deck. At one time this glass-and-steel wall was intended as a primary threshold; now it is merely described as an acoustical shield. In truth, however, one must admit that this late-twentieth-century threshold, like Kahn's porch in Texas, is wonderful because it is, in Kahn's words, "so unnecessary."

Like the buildings that surround the courtyard in one type of traditional Finnish farmhouse, each volume in the science center expresses a distinct function. But in the science center it is not the courtyard but the cylindrical drum of the fourteen-meter-high permanent exhibition hall and the grid of the pillar hall that order the plan.

The building plays a didactic role; it becomes part of the exhibit. The columns of the pillar hall organize the interior on a 9.6-meter grid and provide a rational explanation of the building's weight distribution. Through a system of component columns that increase from a single column at the corners of the building to a double column at the edges and four component columns at the center of the hall, the architects visually describe the increase in load toward the center.

At first glance, the apparently random organization of elements at the edge of chaos is denied by a powerful locus at the center of the rotunda. Here an oculus opens to the sky and Foucault's pendulum inscribes the movement of the earth in a bed of sand. The simultaneous existence of discrete, ordered entities and relations that are fragmented creates an unusual tension that reverberates throughout the science center. All over the building, "harmony at the edge of chaos" resolves itself in forms that are delicately balanced between absolute repose and dynamic tension.

The architects themselves refer to Paul Valéry when they speak of the thoughts that inspired their design. "There are two things that will never cease to threaten the world," Valéry said, "order and disorder." In many ways the Heureka Science Center is a meditation upon this thought.

The building was assembled primarily from prefabricated concrete elements, but some elements, such as the cylindrical drum, were cast in place. Although the science center contains diverse structural systems and a wide range of materials and applications, it was nevertheless completed ahead of schedule and under budget. The fact that Heikkinen and Komonen received Finland's Concrete Structure of the Year Award in 1988 and the Steel Structure Award the next year, both for the Heureka building, attests to the creative energy they spent in the detail and execution of this project.

A nonmaterial component in the architecture that has yet to be constructed is a laser beam linking four ten-meter masts located at the main points of the compass. The beam will form a landmark visible from the aircraft using the nearby Helsinki-Vantaa airport. In addition, a glass spectrum fence, which will refract sunlight into the colors of the rainbow, is planned across the railway and

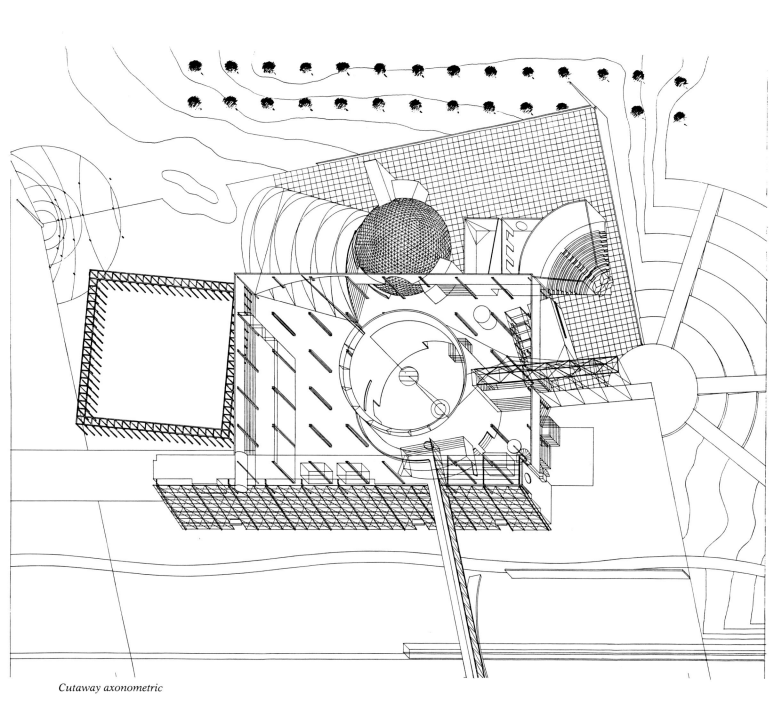

Cutaway axonometric

parallel to the existing spectrum wall.

At times, Heikkinen and Komonen's exploration of the lightness of industrial manufacture and the clarity of a building's assembly vividly recalls the works of Finland's constructivists. The collisions and juxtapositions of volumes within the science center only disguise the fact that its individual elements are often as austere, rational, and minimal as their constructivist predecessors.

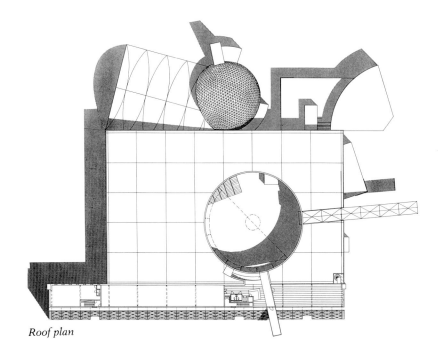

Roof plan

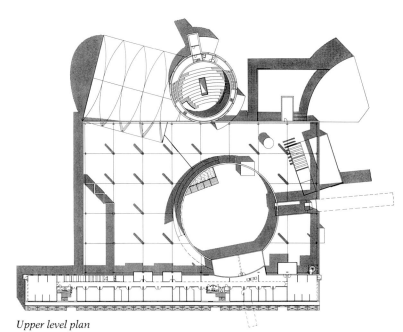

Upper level plan

Ground floor plan

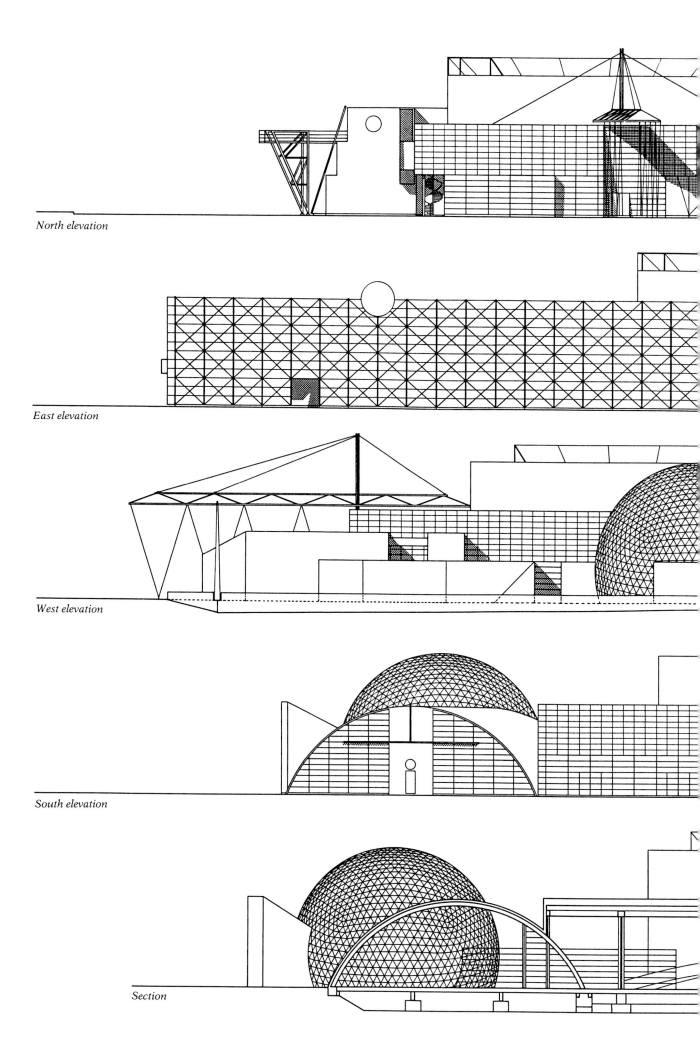

North elevation

East elevation

West elevation

South elevation

Section

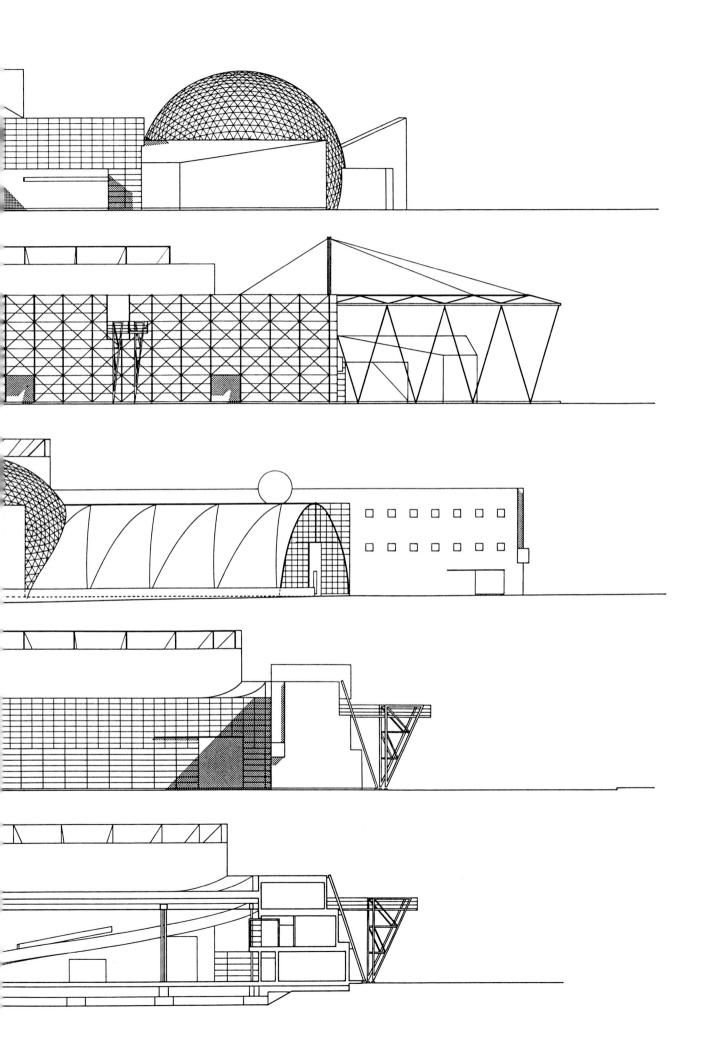

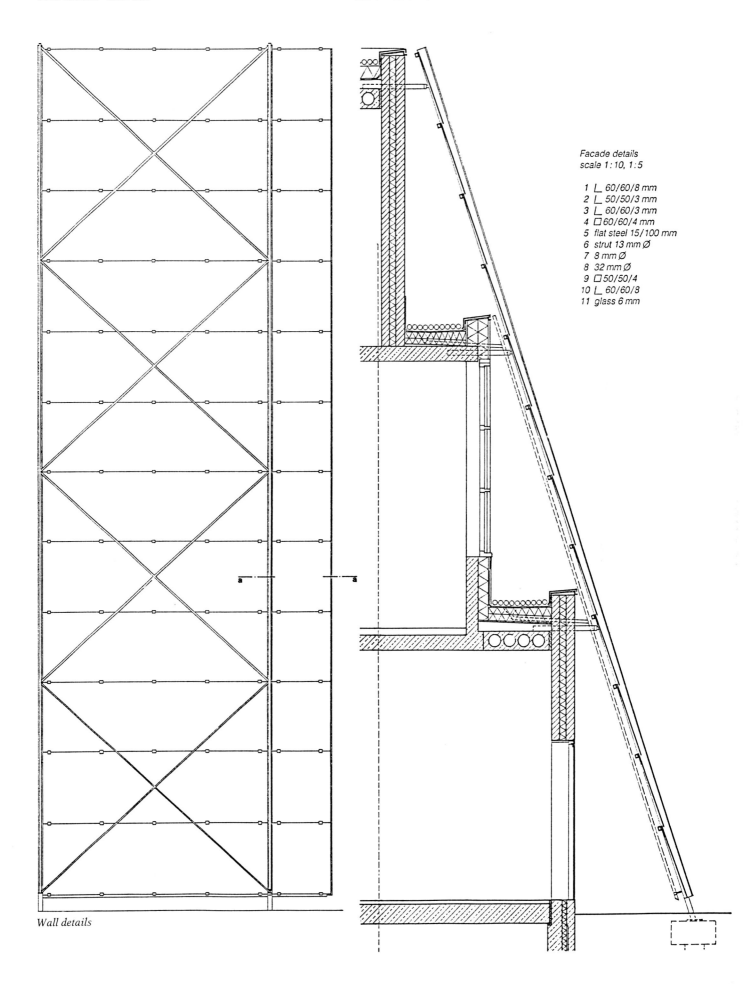

Detail elevation   scale 1:50

Section   scale 1:50

Facade details
scale 1:10, 1:5

1 L 60/60/8 mm
2 L 50/50/3 mm
3 L 60/60/3 mm
4 □ 60/60/4 mm
5 flat steel 15/100 mm
6 strut 13 mm Ø
7 8 mm Ø
8 32 mm Ø
9 □ 50/50/4
10 L 60/60/8
11 glass 6 mm

a ─────────── a

Wall details

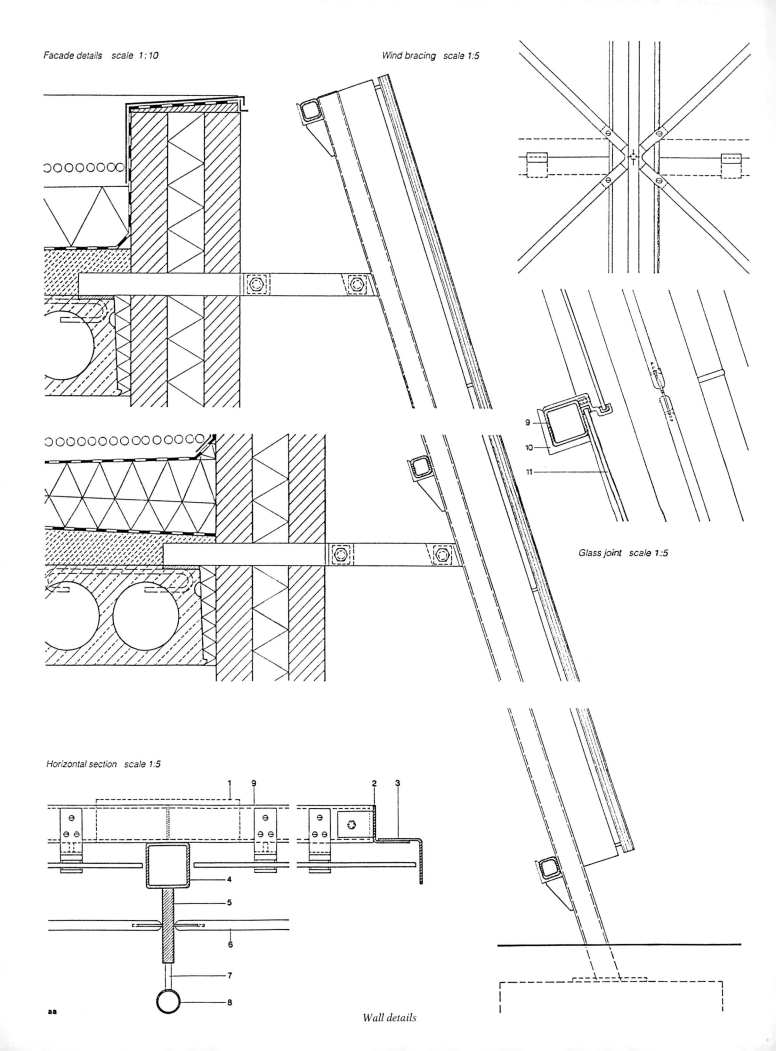

Facade details   scale 1:10

Wind bracing   scale 1:5

Glass joint   scale 1:5

Horizontal section   scale 1:5

1 9   2 3

4

5

6

7

8

aa

Wall details

School for Rescue Operations · Kuopio · 1992

On the vast, horizontal line of earth and water that dominates the Finnish landscape, man-made interventions often appear insignificant. Even today, it is the immense monotony of a consistent tree line and not the buildings that separates earth and sky. In this subarctic landscape even extremes of dark and of light can possess an overwhelming beauty and a frightening sameness. In the school for rescue operations, which trains such personnel as firemen, ambulance drivers, and rescue divers, Heikkinen and Komonen chose to exaggerate the understated qualities of this landscape with a straight line and an arc.

Between the ground and the tree line, the singular gesture of a long, low wall resolutely cuts through the site. This gesture separates untouched nature from a courtyard where the architects shape the earth, plant the trees, and position the rocks. The restraint of this wall and the subdued curve of the dormitory quietly dominate the site while also calling attention to the vastness of the landscape. The way the arc of the auditorium and several

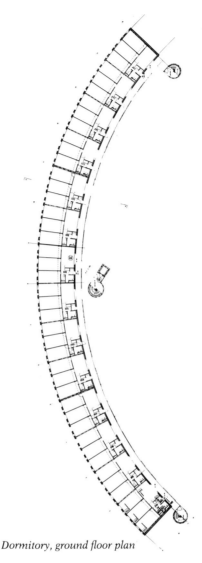

Dormitory, ground floor plan

straight walls intersect at the entry hall reiterates, at the smaller scale of the building, the minimal gestures that mark the larger landscape.

A glass-covered corridor over two hundred meters long connects rooms that contain training areas, storerooms, and an equipment hall holding thirty-one different fire and rescue vehicles. Light is used as an ordering principle in the corridor in two different ways. A lighting beam situated above the glazed roof illuminates the long hall in the darkness, and its long line of light serves as a visual landmark for the neighborhood. The dynamic effect of light is also apparent in the curved dormitory which is lit in the early morning dark as 350 students rush along the steel-mesh enclosed passages on their way to classes.

Heikkinen and Komonen thought that the clear gestures of the school's architecture could provide a framework for the confidence, promptness, prudence, and resolution which are the basis of the professional skills for those who regularly work in chaotic conditions.

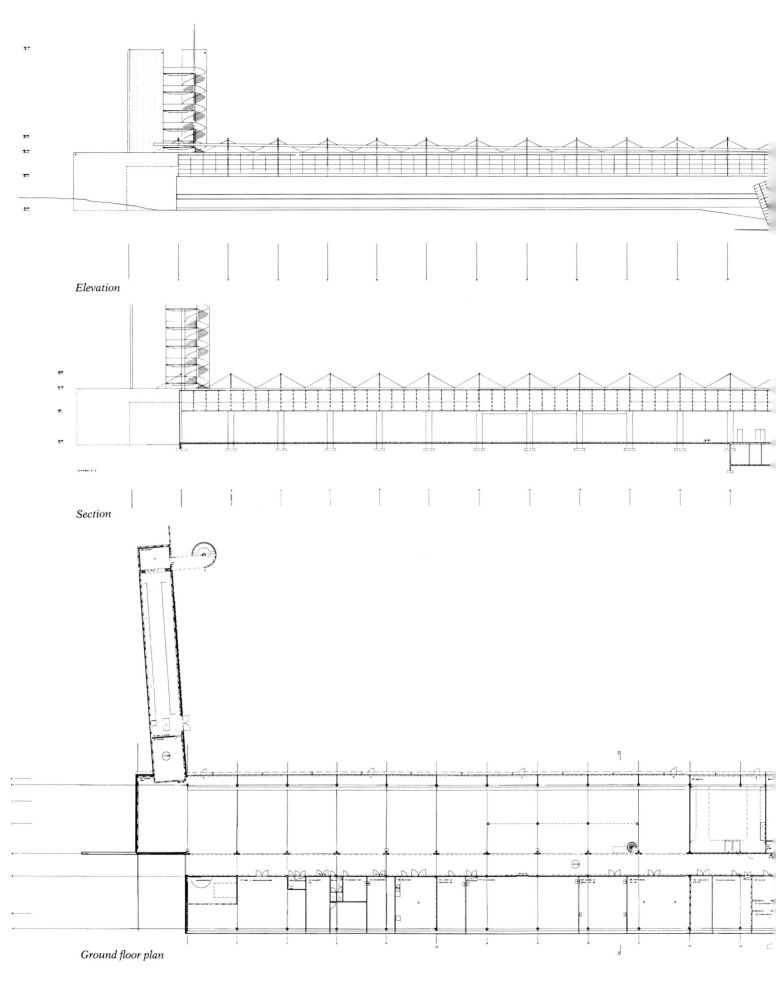

Elevation

Section

Ground floor plan

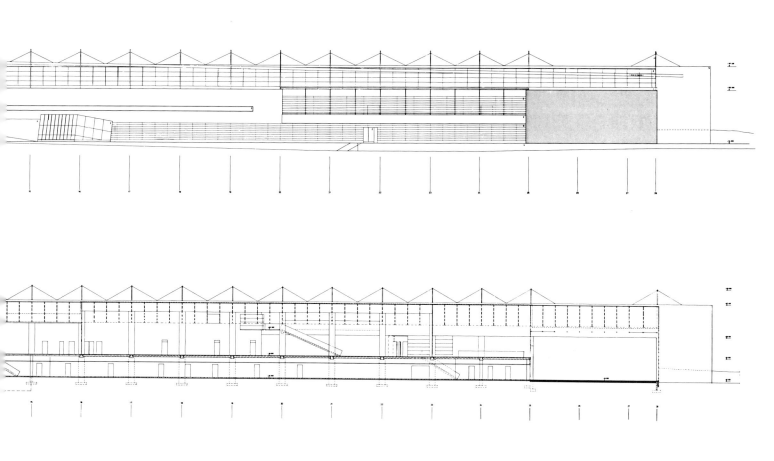

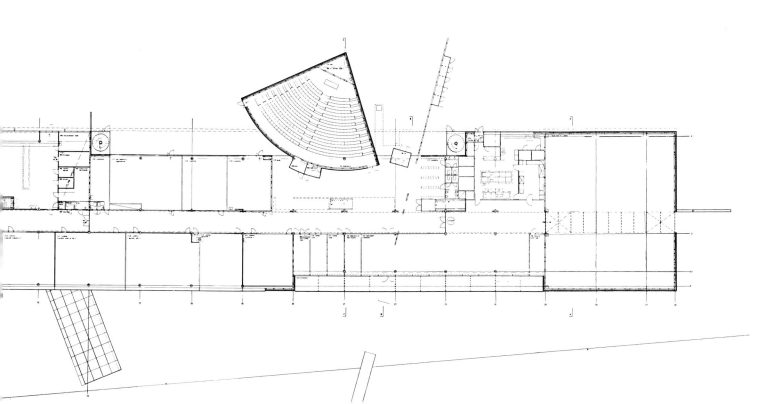

New Airport Building • Rovaniemi • 1992

Aulis Blomstedt once said that design was a matter of stripping away ugliness. Paring away excess has been critical to Heikkinen and Komonen's evolution. Their most recent projects exhibit a confidence in plainness and the economy of simple gesture.

The themes here are the same as those at the Heureka Science Center, but with a new restraint. Relations between an arc and a straight line, a clear structure, a functional organization, and an architectural definition of natural phenomena are all contained within a simple, rectilinear box in the Rovaniemi Airport. Universal aspects of geography and natural phenomena, such as the course of the earth around the sun, were a point of departure for the architecture of the new airport. On the roof of the new building, a narrow, thirty-five-meter-long skylight will locate the line of the polar circle as it was five hundred years ago, thus telling of the variability of this invisible geographical line that still runs through the airfield site.

Another architectural detail that links this unassuming building with cosmic reality is the installation of a fixed mirror on the roof, reflecting the sun's rays

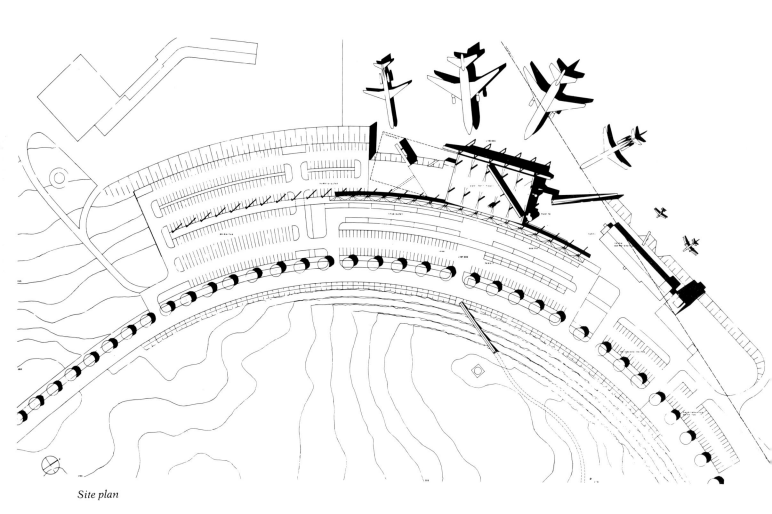

Site plan

onto the hall's floor. During the year, marks registered on the floor at the same time each day will show the sun's declination, illustrating the earth's elliptical orbit with the inscription of an elongated figure eight. The physical manifestation of this natural phenomenon—the sun's analemma—will be explained in as many languages as possible. Initially this description will be in Lapp, but other languages will be added as representatives from other nations arrive at the airport.

The Sun's Analemma installation was designed by the artist Lauri Anttila, who had earlier collaborated with the architects on the Heureka Science Center. Anttila, who is dean of the Finnish Academy of Arts, has aspired, in his words, "to reinstate wisdom in the relationship between man and his environment." He shares with Heikkinen and Komonen a desire to reveal that which is timeless in everyday reality.

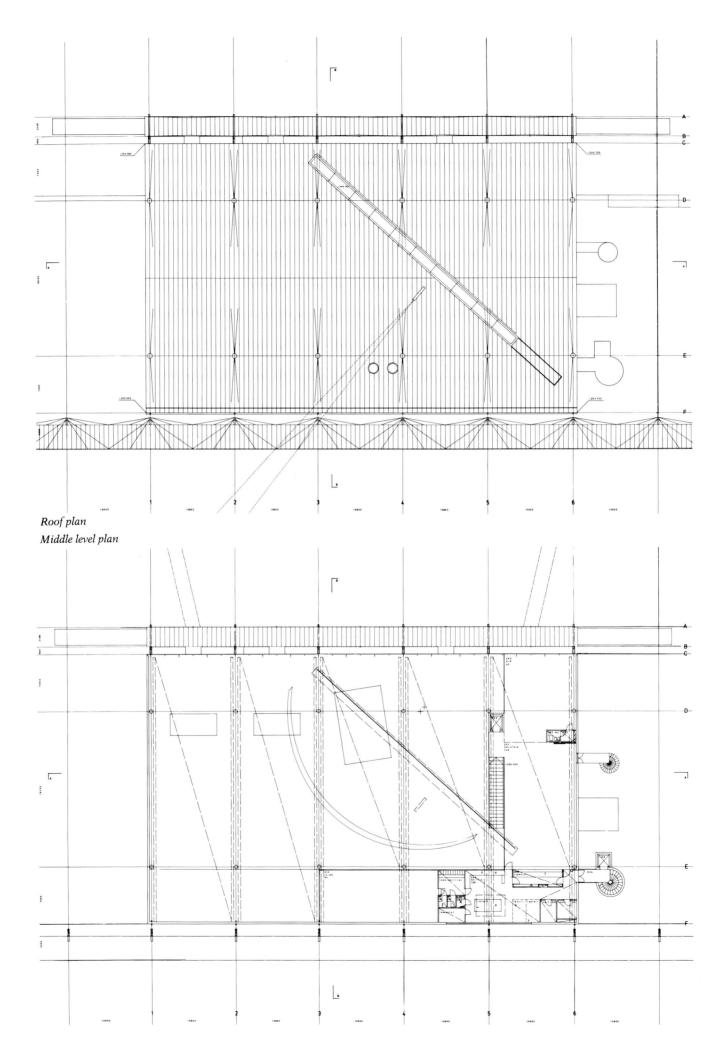

Roof plan

Middle level plan

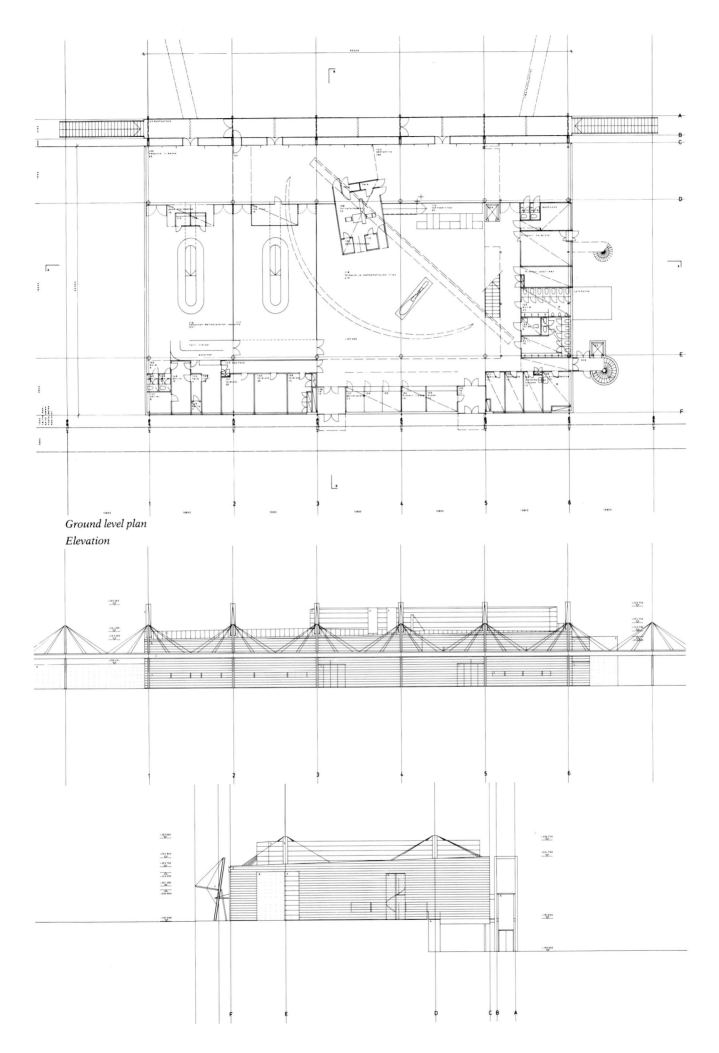

Ground level plan
Elevation

Architecture and Art: Display Pavilion for Sculpture by Martti Aiha • Leeuwarden, Netherlands • 1990

In one regard, Heikkinen and Komonen's most recent architecture is an act of resistance. It suppresses plurality and acknowledges the entity, opposes obscurity with the clarity of construction, and challenges the modern demand for noise with the invisible depths of silence. The exhibition of northern European artists was an opportunity for Heikkinen and Komonen to realize a fragment of the silence that already permeates their latest works, which are just now under construction.

In the summer of 1990 an exhibition entitled "Eleven Cities—Eleven Nations/Contemporary Northern Art and Architecture" was organized in Leeuwarden to consider the north European cultural identity as well as links between architecture and the visual arts. Ten guest artists were chosen from places north of Leeuwarden—Reykjavík, Dublin, Edinburgh, Hamburg, Oslo, Copenhagen, Stockholm, Gdańsk, Tallinn, and Helsinki. Common to all of these cities is the fact that they are in rather small nations and, in some cases, minorities within larger political entities. The exhibition was a chance to highlight local and national feeling and to establish an international link between nations.

Each city was allotted two-hundred-square meters in the Frieslandhaal Exhibition Center. The artists chosen from Finland, sculptor Martti Aiha and architects Mikko Heikkinen and Markku Komonen, began the exhibition with the idea of working separately, but the interaction between them is reflected in the basic design of the pavilion, which was inspired by the sculptor's works, while the sculptor created certain works only after seeing the design for the pavilion.

The architects' description of their project reveals the hidden complexity often found in works of art that are apparently simple:

The basic principle of the architecture was to create visual "acoustics" which would subdue the huge diversity of forms in the exhibition as a whole into a distinct territory for Aiha's works.

In circumstances such as these, buildings or constructions tend to become a kind of architecture in miniature, presenting models of some bigger idea in ersatz materials. We wanted to avoid this and to make our Helsinki pavilion a work of true weight, appearance and size.

Aiha's works are almost exclusively made of wood, and their morphology is complex, like filigree or calligraphy.

The architecture had to be extremely simple. Any dynamism of form or focus on detail would automatically detract from the intensity of the sculptures.

The material chosen was raw steel in two forms: heavy rolled plate, five millimeters thick, and see-through steel mesh.

Six-meter-high plates of steel mesh suspended from the roof of the hall formed the side walls of the exhibition area. Because of the scalelike construction, a person standing in the dark outside the pavilion could see through this mesh wall, though inside, under the lights, he can not. The "roof" of the pavilion was made up of spotlights.

The sculptures were attached to three-meter-high steel slabs whose untreated rolled surfaces offered a background that was both neutral and strong. The supporting structures of the four-hundred-kilo steel plates and their fixtures were concealed in the gap left between each pair of plates.

Uniformity of a singular material and a blank, empty space allowed the architects to create an island of calm and serenity amid the chaos of the other exhibits. Paradoxically, this design, which approaches nothingness, establishes a powerful presence. Its planes of steel mesh acknowledge the presence of the work of art through their utter heedlessness. Amid the stillness of this simple construction Martti Aiha's wood sculptures are given room to become solitary. They are like birds on a wire. Heikkinen and Komonen's background of silence recalls what is so often forgotten in the presentation of a work of art: the loneliness of objects and the solitude of the viewer.

Chancery of Finland • Washington, D.C. • 1993

The site for the Embassy of Finland Chancery is close to an urban structure located adjacent to a park. In this respect, the site resembles a typical condition for a Finnish architect. Building close to nature has encouraged two contrasting traditions in Finnish architecture: a sensual approach that relies on cues directly from nature and an intellectual approach that filters nature through building culture.

Heikkinen and Komonen take the latter approach. The architecture for the chancery relies on an intelligent opposition to nature rather than a romantic encounter.

In plan, a grid of columns structure the site and the building. On the street-side elevation, a metal framework, which acts as a supporting structure for vines, allows the façade to change with the seasons; on the south elevation, it screens the glass wall from the sun and further emphasizes the horizontal pattern of the grid in the vertical dimension. Inside, a tall room slices through the entire length and height of the building, opening the interior to the sky and focusing light on three geometric solids in the hollowed volume. From the double-height interior hall, a grid of columns frames a view of nature, emphasizing the boundary between these two worlds.

According to the architects, the basic principle of the design was to preserve the trees and the natural environment and, at the same time, proportion the scale of the building to the surrounding urban structure. In glass, steel, and Finnish stone, the architects achieve their aim with elegant clarity.

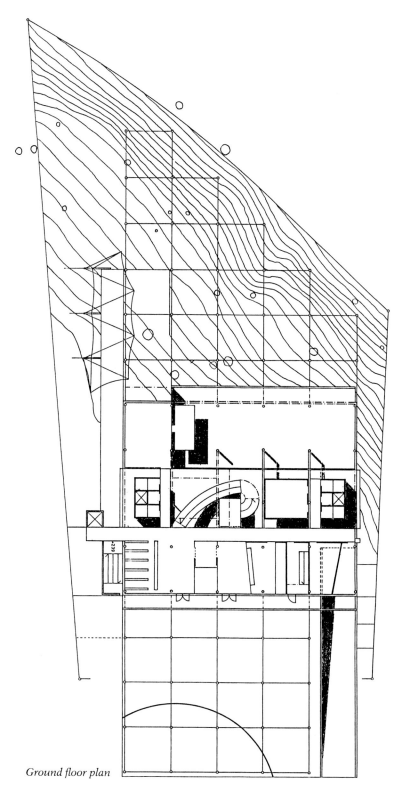

Ground floor plan

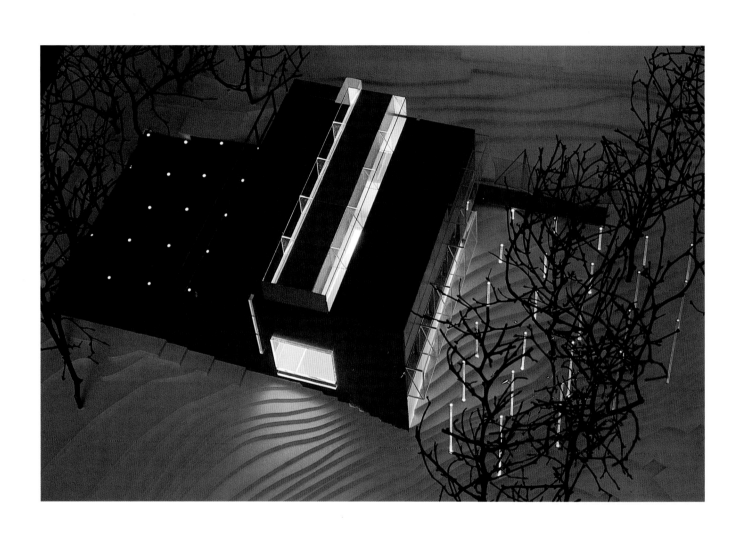

Site plan

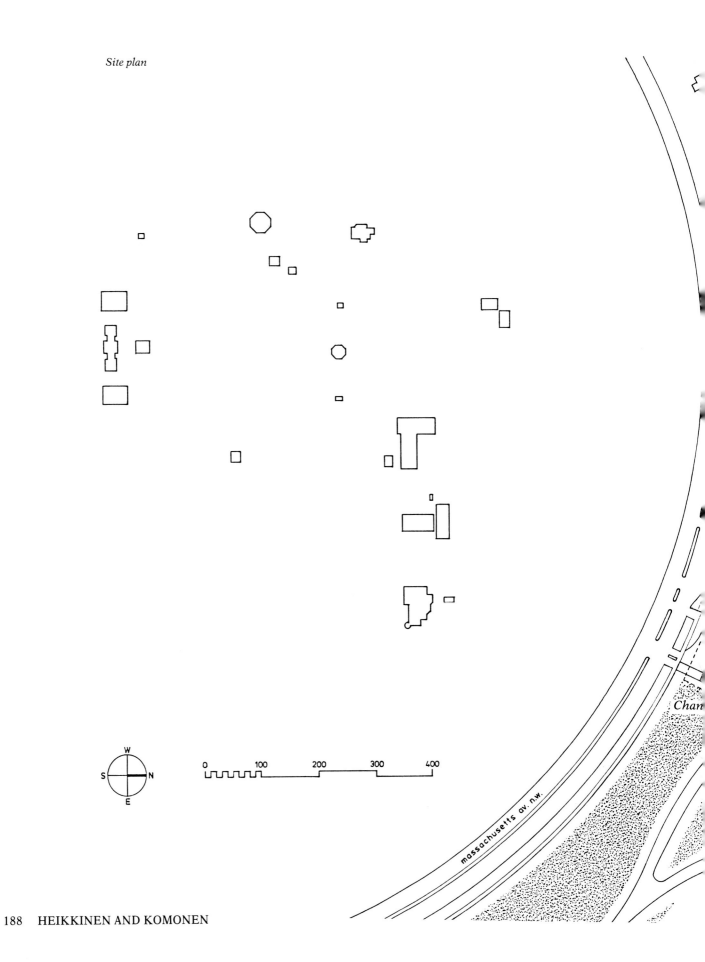

W
S — N
E

0   100   200   300   400

massachusetts av. n.w.

Chan

fulton n.w.

ARRAK

Arctic Circle Visitors' Center Extension • Rovaniemi rural district • 1985

An important aspect of the ARRAK architecture group's work is healing the wounds of the 1960s. In contrast to the prefabricated monotony that characterizes much of the building of that era, their work, according to one of the group's founders, Matti Rautiola, has its basis in regional tradition, the conservation of resources, empathy with the client, and the intention of revitalizing wood construction.

Glass, concrete, and steel were used in addition to wood for the construction of the Arctic Circle Visitors' Center, but wood is most pervasive. Internally, the structure combines concrete slabs, concrete columns, and glue-laminated beams. Storm-felled pine covers the exterior walls.

When Eleanor Roosevelt visited Rovaniemi in 1952, a log cabin was built in her honor on the site. Later, in 1965, another wood-frame structure was built that housed a souvenir shop and a café. The new construction is an extension of the 1965 building, and it is a fascinating study in strange adjacencies. Without ever resorting to indiscriminate contextualism, the new accommodates the old. Traditional methods, such as an old Norwegian technique for ventilating walls, are employed as naturally as modern building

techniques, and they give the new construction a sense of inevitability. It is a harmony that is not easily achieved, but often found in Finland's old wooden houses.

Unlike the interior darkness associated with traditional log construction, the new building is configured to catch the northern light that is so overwhelming in summer and almost nonexistent in winter. Functional components of the visitors' center are individually articulated as volumes along a corridor, and from the exterior these volumes resemble the image of a village more than a singular building. This formal structure recalls both 1930s functionalism and a dominant type of house found in the Finnish countryside—the *porstuba,* or twin cottage—that at once joins and separates. In a new wood building the architects achieve their goal of reordering tradition by simultaneously separating themselves from the past and joining with it.

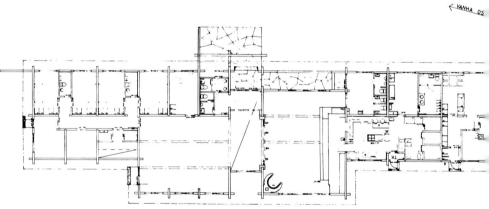

Ground floor plan, original building

Section

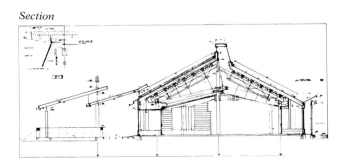

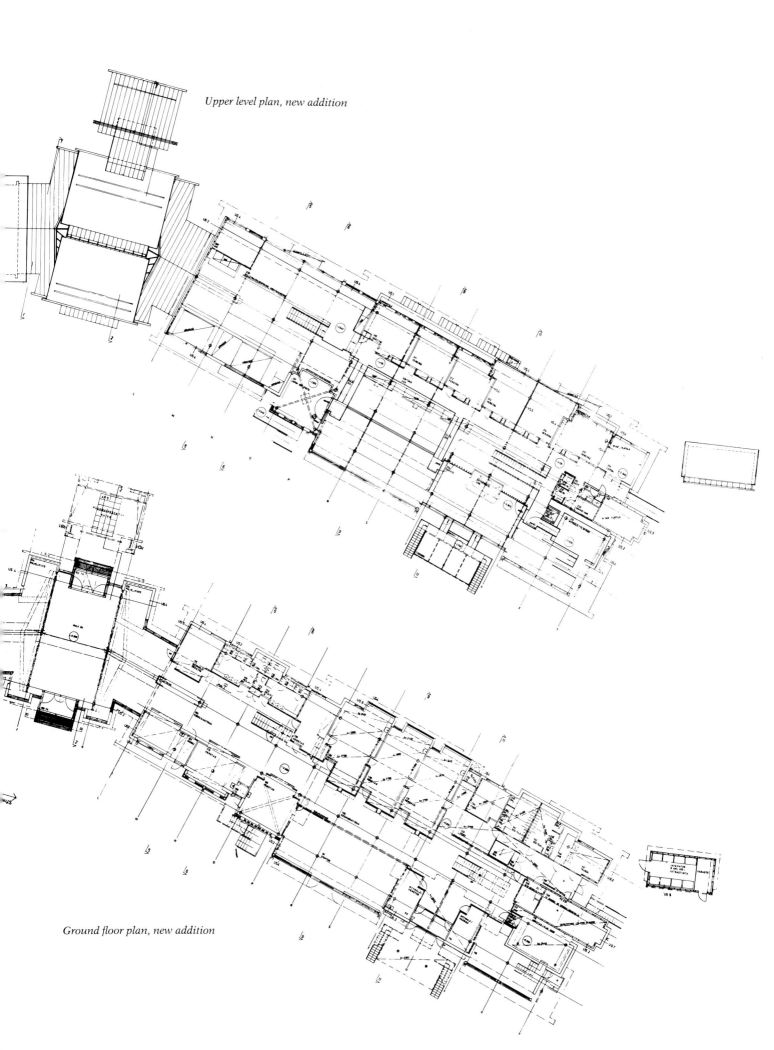

Upper level plan, new addition

Ground floor plan, new addition

Sundial House · Jyväskylä · 1987

Small residential architecture is an exceptional occurrence in modern Finland. Although there is a long tradition of building single-family houses, what has been predominant in Finnish domestic architecture since the 1960s are blocks of low-rise flats, row houses, and terraced housing.

ARRAK's sundial house, commissioned for a housing fair and designed by Hannu Kiiskilä and Harri Hagan, is an experiment in passive solar techniques and the continued feasibility of single-family dwelling. Exploring the technique of wood construction and conservation was one of the architects' primary concerns in the sundial house, as it has been in many of ARRAK's projects over the past ten years.

The house is lifted above the landscape by glue-laminated beams that bear on concrete pillars. Outside walls, ceilings, and the glue-laminated frame are made of prefabricated components, but to describe the house merely in terms of its constituent parts underemphasizes its meticulous construction. Flashing, kerfing, layering, and joining—the simple means of wood building—are essential to this architecture.

ARRAK's work seeks to reveal the means by which a tradition is constructed. Looking at the details of this house one can see centuries of reverence for wood. Every board and structural layer in the sundial house is ventilated. On the roof, the simple line of a yellow snow guard makes manifest the functional and artistic importance of a single wooden board.

ARRAK's architecture can be artistically strong when it cultivates the plainness of peasant buildings. The interior lantern, for example, is built with contemporary wood-building techniques, yet it is a refuge from the alienating sameness that is so often the result of techno-economic efficiency. The novel by-products of industrial culture are missing. This simple room recalls the memory of basic things and their immeasurable qualities.

Plan and section

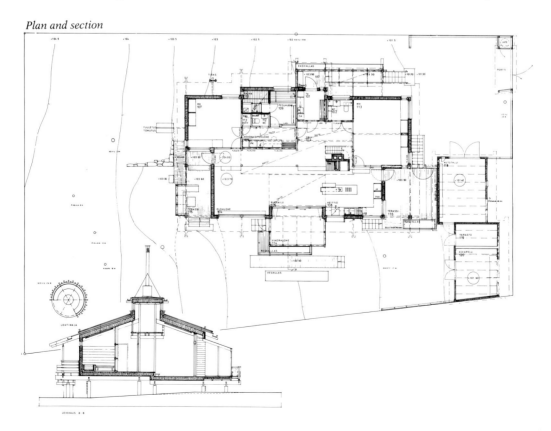

GEORG GROTENFELT

Huitukka Sauna • Juva • 1982

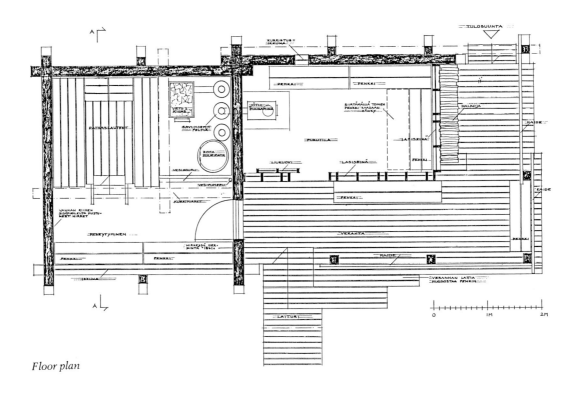

Floor plan

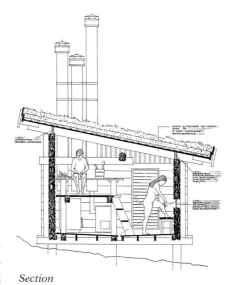

Section

Logs compressed by time and blackened by smoke were salvaged from an old drying barn for the construction of the Huitukka Sauna. Using century-old elements to make a modern building reinforces Georg Grotenfelt's conviction that architecture is a manifestation not only of our time but of earlier generations as well.

He is among the most conservative of his generation. Grotenfelt's architecture begins with Finnish vernacular building customs, the landscape, and an acceptance of the tradition of modernism. The strength and continuity of Finnish culture is the basis for his architectural think-

ing. Even modernism is transformed within the context of regional conditions.

The Savo landscape of eastern Finland and its building customs have been a point of departure for Grotenfelt's early work. His sauna follows the thousand-year-old model of raised benches facing each other adjacent to a wood stove. He believes that the sauna is an almost sacred place, "an enclosed, dark and simple space for the cleansing of the body and soul."

In contrast to the darkness and heavy timber construction of the sauna is a changing room almost completely made of glass

and only held in place by light wood framing. Glass, in this application, is not employed for its material quality, but as a means to see—through transparency and reflection—the texture and configuration of wood in its milled and natural states. Standing in the changing room and looking through a small, square aperture set low to the floor in the back wall, one can see the perpetual contact with earth, water, and trees that characterizes the view from windows in traditional Finnish vernacular buildings.

Grotenfelt approaches architecture as delicately as his sauna touches the Savo landscape. There is always a sense of caution that at any moment his architectural heritage might be lost. So he preserves what he believes to be this last living artifact, bringing the traditional sauna into the present moment. The foundation of his architectural thought is best expressed when he says, "The only possible basis is humility."

Villa Nötterkulla · Inkoo · 1990

On its site in southern Finland, the Villa Nötterkulla and a Bronze-Age burial mound almost touch, but they are separated by a long brick wall and a vast distance in time. This site, with its primitive remnants in the heart of a wooded landscape, was an ideal circumstance for Georg Grotenfelt. When he speaks of a site, he often describes it from an interior point of view—the surrounding landscape. But he also talks of vectors of infinity. Like the work of the Japanese builders he admires, Grotenfelt's architecture often points to something beyond itself; to a particular feature of the landscape, a room's relationship with the morning and evening sun, or an origin in myth or legend. Al-

ways, however, there is a veneration for the old and the forces of nature.

The cultural landscape from which Grotenfelt draws includes modernism filtered through the vernacular. His construction method may at times bear a resemblance to the work of de Stijl, but clear assembly and the autonomy of constituent elements are at least as old as the Lapp hut, which was as easily dismantled as it was put together, and as common as the log construction of Finnish folk architecture.

The spatial organization of the Villa Nötterkulla resembles traditional housing patterns, such as those found in nearby towns like Fagervik. In this traditional

settlement the façades of low-rise houses are grouped in a constant line along a street, but the houses change in elevation, section, and material configuration to give a dynamic quality to the street. Like a river flowing through the town, the houses and street together form an autonomous entity that is separate from the woods, fields, and isolated buildings on either side. In a similar manner, the villa's wall remains constant as the rooms rise and fall, open and close, looking for the sun or a view. Grotenfelt's work is best when it builds upon regional culture, but, as his work evolves, one must wonder how it will confront international civilization.

Ground floor plan

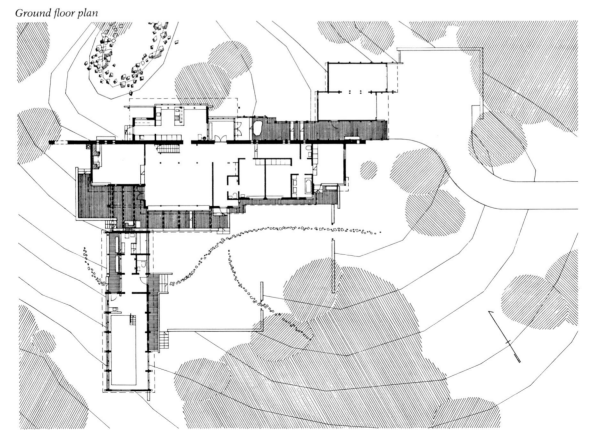

OLLI-PEKKA JOKELA AND PENTTI KAREOJA

Government Office Building • Rauma • 1991

A single line of trees, a long, straight canal leading from the sea one kilometer away, and a pedestrian path along the water provided the setting for Rauma's new government office building. The form of Jokela and Kareoja's building is as clear as the vivid characteristics of the site. Twenty-three columns, a 144-meter-long wall, and an equally long interior passage mirror, separate, and merge with the trees and water along the canal.

Inside the building a narrow three-story gallery space opens to the sky and reflects the strong linear order that begins at the canal. Offices, located along two

balconies, open to the interior gallery and reinforce the notion of street. At the gallery level, public rooms are hierarchically differentiated with two court halls and a curvilinear room for civil weddings located outside the passage, on the banks of the canal. Near the center of the gallery water flows under the building to make a light-reflecting surface that adds to the tranquility of the courtyard side and reinforces the maritime character of the town.

The new government offices by Jokela and Kareoja will become a critical intervention in the town of Rauma. In a bleak 1970s suburb, the new building offers a

direction for developing an urban fabric. It is a reminder that modern architecture can be made with relatively simple means and the same clarity of thought that gave integrity and authenticity to the old wooden structures found within the dense urban configuration of Rauma's medieval town plan.

Originally the building crossed the canal and was conceived more as a city gate than as a fragment of a city wall, which it eventually became in the second stage of the competition. Although the competition project initially exceeded the budget, the design raised doubts about the correctness of established cost levels for government office buildings. Ultimately the building was slightly modified to meet the budget, but the budget was also raised to meet the architecture.

As a model for a more humane type of office building, Jokela and Kareoja's design is a distinct move away from the alienating labyrinth of fluorescent uniformity that characterizes the modern office.

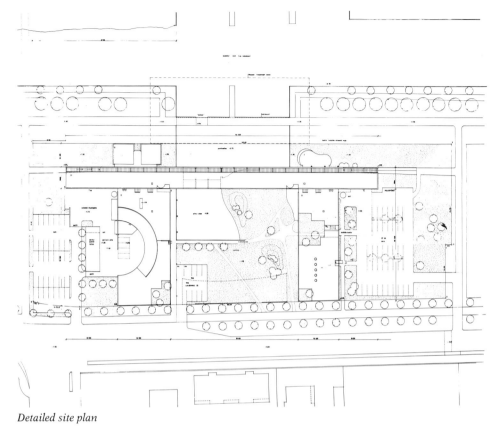

Detailed site plan

Site plan

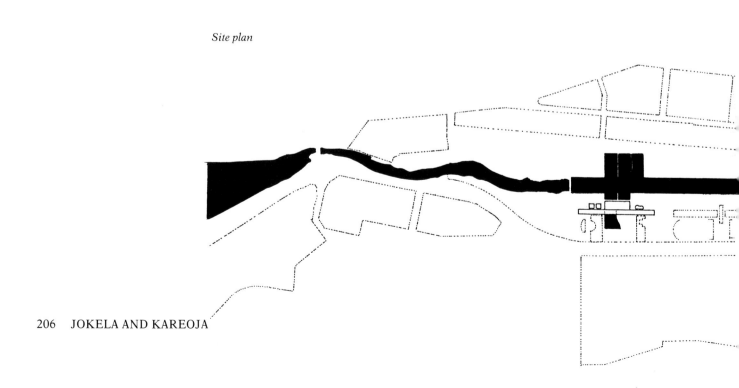

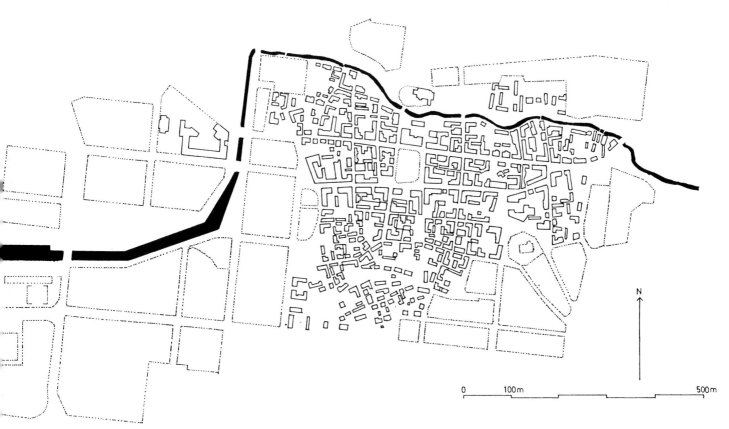

0   100m   500m

N

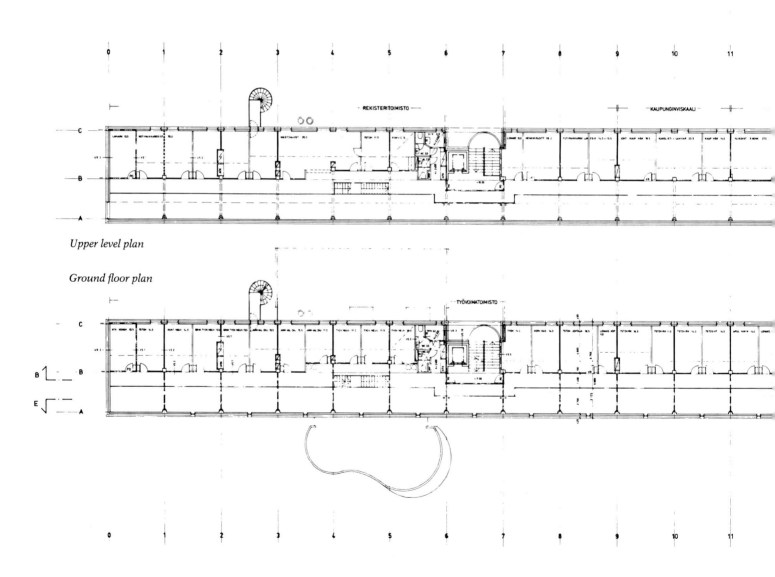

Upper level plan

Ground floor plan

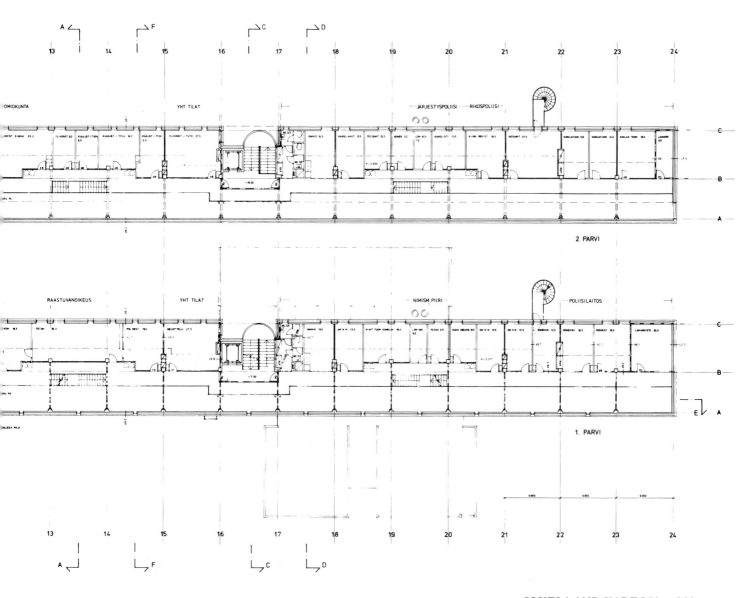

2. PARVI

1. PARVI

Hämeenkylä Church • Vantaa • 1992

One of the most important decisions Jokela and Kareoja made in their design for the Hämeenkylä Church was building up the site by three meters. It gave the architects the opportunity to make a stair separating the courtyard entrance of the church from the street.

Where the existing parish hall had no more presence than its disordered surroundings, the new architecture controls the site and acts as a center for this small valley. The fortresslike brick wall of the church and the bell tower establish tension in the composition, allowing the stair to anticipate a place of arrival. Wall,

tower, and stair are precisely the elements Aalto used to make the entry for the town hall in Säynätsalo; he too built up the site three meters to make a courtyard. But here there is no abrupt change in scale. From the grounds outside the church to the courtyard, the proportions remain grand.

The procession to the church begins at the bottom of the exterior stair and ends at the altar. In between are three entries and three rooms: a monumental portal, a small, gatelike threshold, and a large glass wall lead in succession to the courtyard, the entry hall, and the sacred room of the church. Along the route one

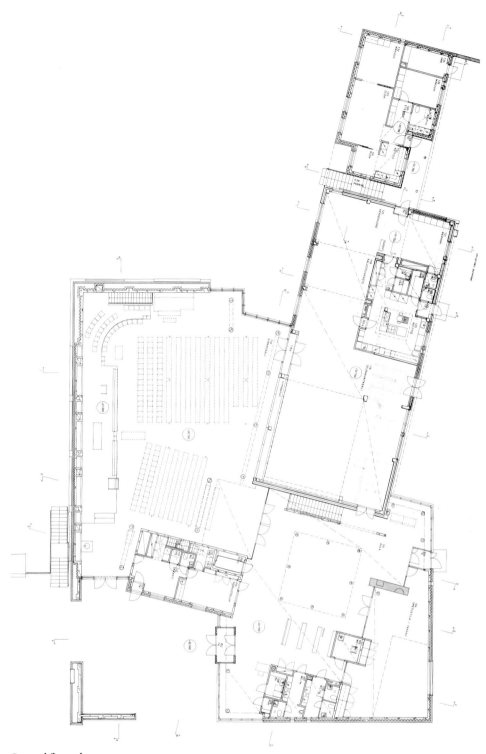

Ground floor plan

passes the tower and hears the toll of the bells. As one enters the vestibule, the west corner opens to a view of the cemetery and the presence of death. At the altar the churchgoers are almost where they began—they have come in a circle and are only separated from the entry stair by an immense wall. That wall, facing southeast, is constructed in such a way that the interior of the church, in the architect's words, "lives with light."

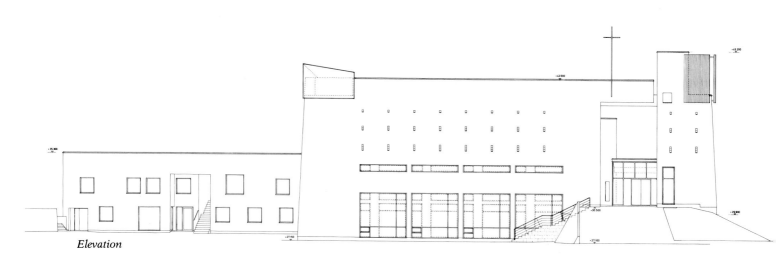

Elevation

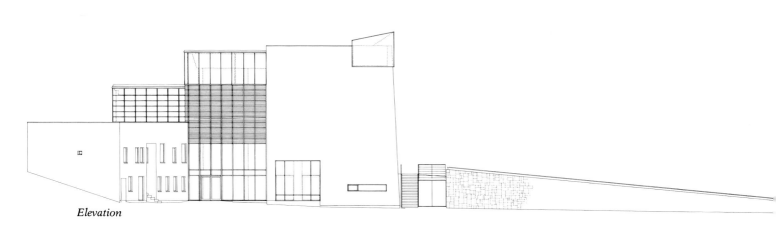

Elevation

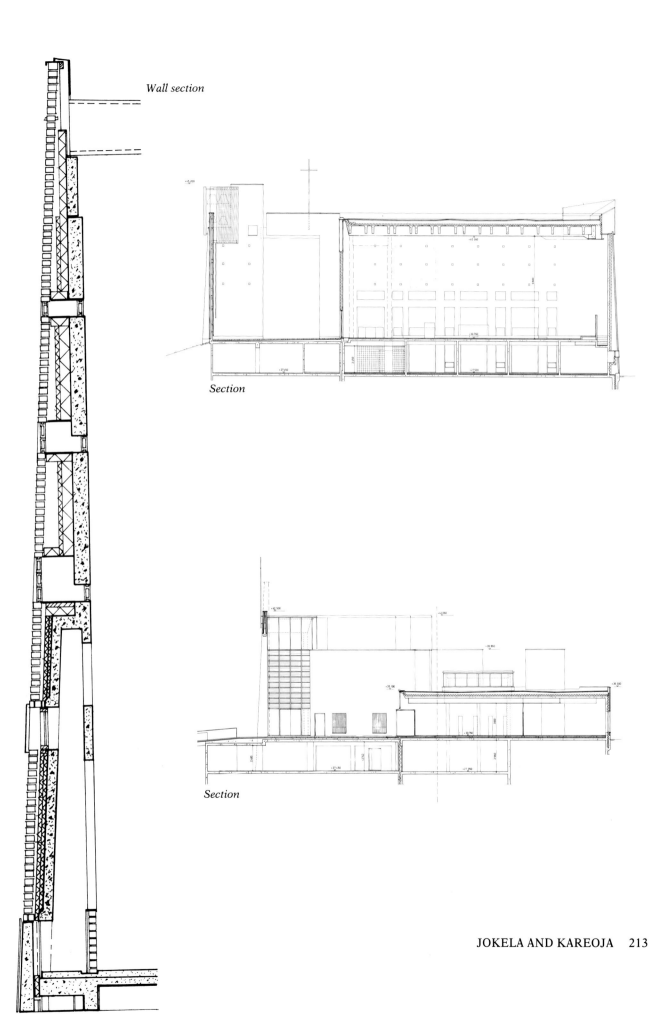

Wall section

Section

Section

MONARK

Finnish 1992 World Exhibition Pavilion • Seville • 1991

World's fair pavilions have been critical to the careers of three of Finland's most prominent architects in this century—Eliel Saarinen, Alvar Aalto, and Reima Pietilä. Each designer has given vivid expression to a particular aspect of Finnish architecture, and each pavilion has raised the international reputation of Finnish design.

In 1900, at the Paris World's Fair, Herman Gesellius, Armas Lindgren, and Eliel Saarinen aspired to architecture as a total work of art in a pavilion that linked Finland's national identity with turn-of-the-century romanticism.

One might have thought that the whole of Finnish life was wood, judging from the sensual expression of Alvar Aalto's world exhibition pavilions in Paris in 1937 and New York in 1939. The dynamic architectural form of these pavilions, and in particular the interior at New York, brought Aalto and the sensuous element of Finnish architecture to the center of international attention.

Oddly enough, it was Reima Pietilä's pavilion for the Brussels World's Fair in 1958 that displayed the rational and constructive approach that was to dominate architectural thinking for over a generation in Finland, even

"Helvetinkolu"

though he later abandoned these thoughts as his work moved increasingly toward regionalism and expressionism.

The most recent Finnish design for a world-exhibition pavilion synthesizes aspects of Finnish architecture that are at once bound to national culture and to a desire for universality. The utter simplicity of the pavilion clarifies the architectural idea. Between the flat plane of cold gray steel and the sensual volume of Finnish pine there is a chasm of opposing qualities. The efficient metal "machine" is precise, like a mathematical calculation, almost formless: it is an instrument that is useful, like a tool. On the other side of the rift, the curvilinear "keel" is pregnant with smells and memories associated with traditional wood buildings. It recalls centuries of Finnish vernacular constructions that were without pretension. Together, these two entities form a space of silence. Considered restraint, elemental purity, and minimalism afford this gesture maximum artistic effect.

As lucid as the architecture itself is the architects' description

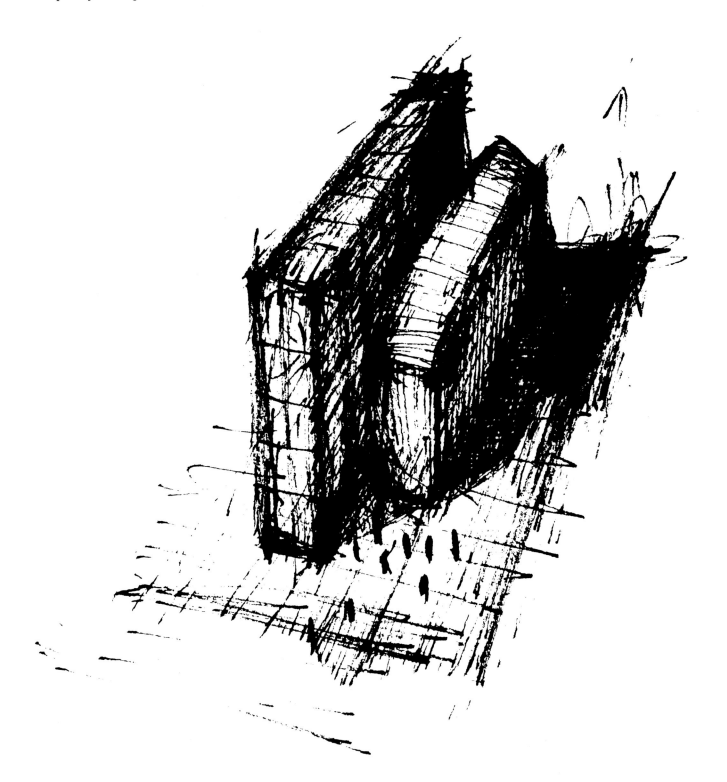

of their project:

Instead of one building, Finland's World's Exhibition Pavilion is two buildings. . . . One, named Keel, is made of wood—Finnish pine. The construction principles follow the traditional way of building wooden ships.

A bearing glue-lam skeleton is covered with boards on both walls and roof. Floors are planks nailed together. The whole building is handcrafted and smells of Finnish charcoal tar.

The other building, named Machine, is made of steel. This building has a character of industralized culture. Totally modular and carefully fabricated, Machine is quick to erect and disassemble.

Machine has a modular size of 4,000 x 4,000 x 6,000 millimeters. The steel primary structure and the floor panels, windows and facades follow this scheme.

A six-millimeter-thick steel skin covers Machine. The steel sheets are cold-rolled and lacquered.

When a window occurs behind the skin, the steel sheet is perforated. The exhibition itself is also of a dual nature. There is an exhibition in Machine and an exhibition in Keel.

The main thing in the Finnish Pavilion is not the buildings themselves but the space between them. Keel and Machine create between them a long, narrow shaft—fifteen meters high and thirty-five meters long but only two meters in width.

This primary idea of the pavilion comes from central Finland, near Ruovesi. In the middle of that wilderness can be found a place where the rock has split into two parts through natural forces.

In old Finnish superstition people feared and worshipped this place. They named it the Shaft of Hell.

Entrance to the pavilion is made via a ramp in the shaft between Machine and Keel. Visitors move slowly upward in tension between nature and technology, gradually experiencing the coexistence of regional and international worlds.

Like Gesellius, Lindgren, and Saarinen, who designed Finland's first world exhibition pavilion over ninety years ago, not one of the architects in the MONARK group was over twenty-five years old during the building's initial design. In fact, at the time of the competition, one architect in the group, Jari Tirkkonen, was working in the office of Kristian Gullichsen; another, Juha Jääskelainnen, was working with Juhani Pallasmaa's office; and several of the designers had been recent students in Mikko Heikkinen's design studio at the Helsinki University of Technology.

It is refreshing, in a time when so much good architecture is crushed by bad faith, to see a national still willing to trust its world image to young talent.

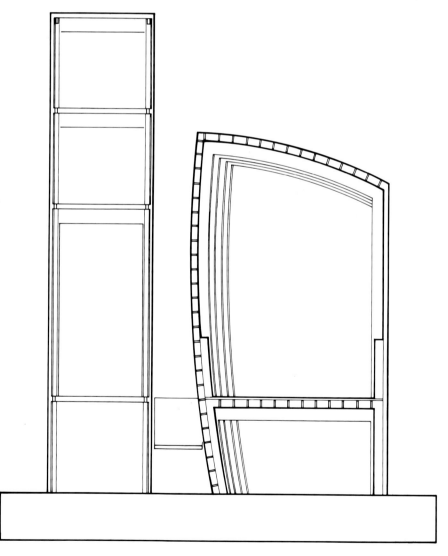

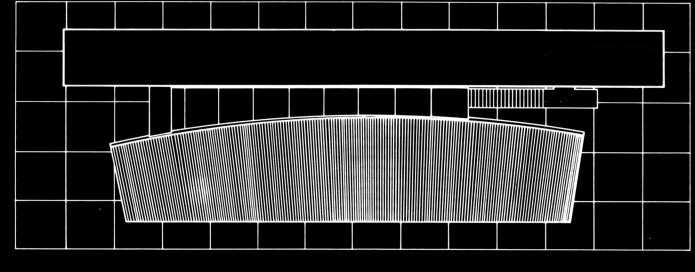

Master plan

Upper level plan

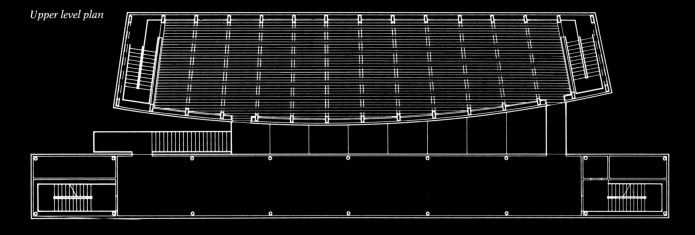

Ground floor plan

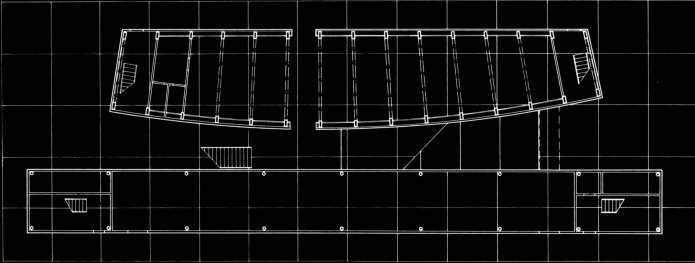

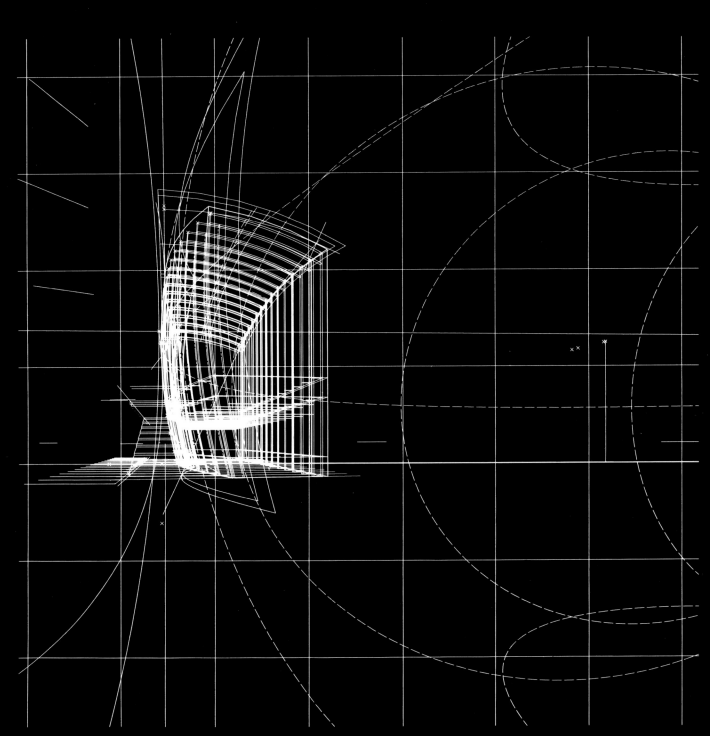

Computer-aided design study

Architects' Biographies

Arkkitehdit Ky • Gullichsen-Kairamo-Vormala
Founded in 1973, Arkkitehdit Ky won the State Award for Architecture and Community Planning in 1978.

Kristian Gullichsen
—Born in 1932
—Graduated Helsinki University of Technology, 1960
—Head, Exhibitions Office of the Museum of Finnish Architecture, 1965–67
—Own office, 1961–73
—Milieu Prize of the journal *Uusi Suomi*, 1989
—Concrete Structure of the Year Prize, 1990
—State Artist Professor, 1988–93

Erkki Kairamo
—Born in 1936
—Graduated Helsinki University of Technology, 1963
—Own office, 1963–73
—Finnish State Award for Architecture, 1978
—Three-year state scholarship for artists, 1981
—Steel Structure of the Year Prize, 1984

Timo Vormala
—Born in 1942
—Graduated Helsinki University of Technology, 1971
—Lecturer, Helsinki University of Technology, 1978

ARRAK Architects
Matti Rautiola
—Born in 1950
—Graduated Tampere University of Technology, 1975
—Partner of ARRAK, 1976
—Assistant Professor, Tampere University of Technology, Department of Architecture, 1976–83

Hannu Kiiskilä
—Born 1950
—Graduated Tampere University of Technology, 1978
—Partner of ARRAK, 1976
—Assistant Professor, Tampere University of Technology, Department of Architecture, 1980–85

Harri Hagan
—Born in 1948
—Graduated Tampere University of Technology, 1983
—Employed in the offices of Hagan Ltd, Pori, 1970–80; Aarne Ehojoki, Turku, 1978; Helmer Löfström, Helsinki, 1980–82; ARRAK, 1983

Esko Rautiola
—Born in 1955
—Graduated Tampere University of Technology, 1985
—Partner of ARRAK, 1976

Asko Kinnunen
—Born in 1951
—Graduated Tampere University of Technology, 1976
—Assistant Professor, Tampere University of Technology, Department of Architecture, 1979–83

Georg Grotenfelt
—Born in 1951
—Graduated Helsinki University of Technology, 1980
—Worked in the office of Kari Järvinen
—Own office from 1980
—State scholarship for artists, 1988

Heikkinen and Komonen
Heikkinen and Komonen set up their office in 1974 and won the State Award for Architecture and Community Planning in 1989. They won the Concrete Structure of the Year Prize in 1988 and the Steel Structure of the Year Prize in 1989. In 1990 they received the Quaternario Award in Venice.

Mikko Heikkinen
—Born in 1949
—Graduated Helsinki University of Technology, 1975
—Employed in the offices of Kristian Gullichsen, Söderlund-Valovirta, A-Konsultit, 1969–86
—State scholarship for artists, 1989

Markku Komonen
—Born in 1945
—Graduated Helsinki University of Technology, 1974
—Editor in chief of *Arkkitehti*, 1977–81
—Head, Exhibitions Office of the Museum of Finnish Architecture, 1978–86
—Collaborated with Juhani Pallasmaa, 1966–72
—Three-year State Scholarship, 1988–90

Helin and Siitonen
Helin and Siitonen won the Viljo Revell Fund Award in 1973 and went into partnership in 1979. They won the State Award for Architecture and Community Planning in 1983.

Pekka Helin
—Born in 1945
—Graduated Helsinki University of Technology, 1971
—Partner in the office of Katras, 1971–79

Tuomo Siitonen
—Born in 1946
—Graduated Helsinki University of Technology, 1972
—Partner in the office of Katras, 1971–79

Jokela and Kareoja
Jokela and Kareoja opened their practice in 1987. They won first prizes in four architectural competitions from 1986 to 1989.

Olli-Pekka Jokela
—Born in 1955
—Graduated Helsinki University of Technology, 1982
—Employed in the offices of Heikki and Kaija Sirén, 1977–80; Kaarina Löfström and Matti K. Mäkinen, 1981–82; Vilhelm Helander and Juha Leiviskä, 1982–86

Pentti Kareoja
—Born in 1959
—Graduated Tampere University of Technology, 1988
—Employed in the offices of Kirsti and Erkki Helamaa, 1982–83; Kevin Roche, 1984; Henrik and Kai Wartiainen, 1985–86

Järvinen and Airas
Järvinen and Airas opened their office in 1973 and won the State Award for Architecture and Community Planning in 1986.

Kari Järvinen
—Born in 1940
—Graduated Helsinki University of Technology, 1967
—Employed in the office of Bertel Saarnio, 1962–69

Timo Airas
—Born in 1947
—Graduated Helsinki University of Technology, 1983
—Employed at the Museum of Finnish Architecture, 1969–73

Juha Leiviskä

—Born in 1936
—Graduated Helsinki University of Technology, 1963
—Founded his own office in 1967 and together with Vilhelm Helander from 1978
—State Scholarship for Artists, 1973
—Väinö Vähäkallio scholarship, 1967
—State Award for Architecture and Community Planning, 1982

MONARK

Juha Kaakko
—Born in 1964
—Architecture student, Helsinki University of Technology
—Employed in the offices of Olli Parviainen and Risto Kaakko

Juha Jääskelainnen
—Born in 1966
—Architecture student, Helsinki University of Technology
—Employed in the office of Juhani Pallasmaa, 1988–89

Petri Rouhianen
—Born in 1966
—Architecture student, Helsinki University of Technology
—Employed in the office of Kai Lohman

Matti Sanaksenaho
—Born in 1966
—Architecture student, Helsinki University of Technology
—Employed in the office of Kai Wartiainen, 1988–89

Jarl Tirkkonen
—Born in 1965
—Architecture student, Helsinki University of Technology
—Employed in the office of Arkkitehdit Ky•Gullichsen-Kairamo-Vormala, 1988–89

Juhani Pallasmaa

—Born in 1936
—Graduated Helsinki University of Technology, 1966
—Partner, K. Mikkola-J. Pallasmaa, 1963–67; 1975–78
—Partner, Juutilainen-Kairamo-Mikkola-Pallasmaa, 1966–72
—Partner, K. Mikkola-J. Pallasmaa, 1976–80
—Own office, 1983
—Director, Institute of Industrial Arts, Helsinki, 1970–72
—Head, Exhibitions Office of the Museum of Finnish Architecture, 1968–72 and 1974–78
—Director, Museum of Finnish Architecture, Helsinki, 1978–83
—State Artist Professor, 1983–88
—Honorary Fellow, American Institute of Architects, 1989

Aarno Ruusuvuori

—Born in 1925
—Graduated Helsinki University of Technology, 1951
—Own office since 1952
—Helsinki University of Technology: Assistant Professor of Architecture, 1952–59, Acting Professor of Architecture, 1959–63, Professor of Architecture, 1963–66
—Väinö Vähäkallio Award, 1955
—Lindahl-Thomé Award, 1955
—Kordelin Award, 1957
—State Scholarship for Artists, 1970 and 1973–75
—Northern Scholar, Edinburgh University, Scotland, 1980
—Honorary Fellow, American Institute of Architects, 1982
—State Artist Professor, 1978–83
—Director, Museum of Finnish Architecture, Helsinki, 1975–78 and 1983–88

Arto Sipinen

—Born in 1936
—Graduated Helsinki University of Technology, 1961
—Own office since 1965
—Viljo Revell Memorial Prize, 1969
—Jyväskylä University Medal, 1973
—State Scholarship for Artists, 1983–85

Eero Valjakka

—Born in 1937
—Graduated Helsinki University of Technology
—Own office since 1985
—State Award for Architecture and Community Planning, 1975

Illustration Credits